a guide to
MEXICAN
HISTORY

by

PAULINE R. KIBBE

So long as time shall exist,
So long as the earth shall last,
Your fame will endure,
Your glory will persist,
México-Tenochtitlan.

from Brief Memorial on the Founding of Colhuacan

TITLES IN THE MINUTIAE MEXICANA SERIES

A Flower Lover's Guide to Mexico
A Bird Watcher's Guide to Mexico
A Guide to Mexican Mammals & Reptiles
A Guide to Mexican Archaeology
A Guide to Mexican Witchcraft
A Guide to Mexican History
A Guide to Tequila, Mezcal and Pulque
A Guide to Mexican Poetry, Ancient and Modern
A Guide to Architecture in Ancient Mexico
A Guide to Mexican Ceramics
Minute Guide to Speaking Spanish
For the Love of Mexico
Mexican Recipes and Memories, Too

INDIAN PEOPLES OF MEXICO SERIES

The Maya World
The Aztecs Then and Now
The Great Temple and The Aztec Gods
Oaxaca, the Archaeological Record

Sixteenth printing ... August, 1991

Derechos reservados conforme a la ley © *1964, 1974, 1978, 1983*

ISBN 968-7074-06-X Doceava edición revisada y corregida
ISBN 968-7074-00-00 Oncena edición

Editorial MINUTIAE MEXICANA, S. A. de C. V.
Insurgentes Centro 114-210; 06030 México, D. F.;
Tel. 535-9488

There are many representations of Quetzalcoatl, a god ancient in Middle America before the Christian era began. We have adopted as the insignia of our series the most common — that of the feathered serpent. The father and creator of man, Quetzalcoatl was the beneficent god of life and the wind, the god of civilization who inspired man to study the stars, to develop agriculture, industry and the arts.

Impreso y hecho en México

"It's the little things that count." And that is precisely the reason for Minutiae Mexicana's existence.

Interesting details, curious sidelights, little-known facts are the key to the understanding and enjoyment of a country and its people.

M. M. editors have long felt that Mexico has lacked qualified interpreters abroad. We consider as qualified those Mexicans who are experts in their respective fields, or foreigners who have lived and worked in Mexico long enough to absorb its essence, and who can transmit their experiences with a feeling for and knowledge of cause and effect—in short, integrated observers.

Brief though it may be, each volume in the series represents a synthesis of many years of interest and awareness. Some volumes are serious, others light; all are as honest, accurate and informative as we can make them... to the reader's profit and ours, we hope.

The number of people within and outside of Mexico who have helped and encouraged us in this project is as huge as it has been heartening, but to one person we would like to pay special tribute — Lic. Alfonso de Rosenzweig-Díaz, a member of the Mexican Diplomatic Corps for half a century. As Ambassador to England during World War II, he spent many hours in London bomb shelters, and there he remembered his homeland — those interesting details, curious sidelights and little-known facts — culminating in a work of tremendous scholarship and research, *La Mexicanidad de México*. His interest and example were a deciding force in bringing this series into being.

The Editors

TABLE OF CONTENTS

ART: Oluf Olsen and Alberto Beltrán

COVER DESIGN: Mexico City's soaring skyscraper, the Latin American Tower, viewed through the door of an ancient Maya temple symbolizes not only Mexico's history from pre-Conquest times to the hum and bustle of today's modernity, but also the fact that modern Mexico lives with its glorious past as a constant companion.

SETTING THE STAGE

The Republic of Mexico is the United States' next-door neighbor on the south. More than half the border between the two countries, from El Paso to Brownsville, Texas, is defined by the Río Grande. West of El Paso no such natural boundary exists, and only an imaginary line separates Mexico from New Mexico, Arizona and California.

Roughly triangular in form, narrowing from its broad base, some 1,600 miles in length, at the U. S. border to a width of merely 125 miles at the Isthmus of Tehuantepec, Mexico has an area of 760,373 square miles. Among Latin American republics, only Brazil and Argentina are larger. It is divided into 32 political units: 31 states and the Federal District which, like the District of Columbia in the United States, is the seat of the national government.

On the west and south Mexico is bounded by the Pacific Ocean; on the southeast by Guatemala, Belize and the Caribbean Sea; and on the east by the Gulf of Mexico. The peninsula of Baja California, 760 miles long, is separated from the mainland by the Gulf of California.

Mexico possesses 6,212 miles of coastline, 4,438 on the west and south, 1,774 on the east.

It is a mountainous country, two-thirds of its total area being occupied by mountains from 3,000 to 18,000 feet in height. The two principal ranges are the Sierra Madre Occidental, which runs down the western side of Mexico, and the Sierra Madre Oriental, on the eastern side.

These two ranges turn inland and join a few miles south of Mexico City. In this east-west jumble of mountains are to be found the lofty peaks, many of them extinct volcanoes, that give the Mexican landscape its special character. Highest of them all is the Pico de Orizaba, in the state of Veracruz, 18,855 feet high; and the most famous are Popocatepetl, "Hill that Smokes," and Iztaccihuatl, "White Woman," both over 17,000 feet, and both straddling the line between the states of Mexico and Puebla. In all, there are 22 Mexican peaks that tower 10,000 feet or more above sea level.

Cradled between the two Sierra Madre ranges is a vast tableland, likewise triangular in shape, criss-crossed by lower mountain chains. In fact, the central part of the country consists of a series of valleys walled in by mountains.

This is where the majority of Mexico's 84 million (1990 estimate) inhabitants live: on the mountain slopes and in the mountain valleys of the Central Plateau. The coastal plains are hot and humid. The broad northern desert regions of Sonora, Chihuahua, Coahuila, Nuevo León and Tamaulipas are hot and arid in summer, sometimes bitterly cold in winter. The peninsula of Yucatán is an almost barren limestone plain to the north, steaming jungle to the south. Tropical, too, is much of Campeche, Chiapas, Tabasco and Oaxaca, in the south.

Because the Tropic of Cancer passes through the center of the country, it might be supposed that Mexico's climate is uniformly hot. But the altitude of the central highlands creates a year-round temperate climate without extremes of either heat or cold. There

Popocatepetl looms majestically over Tlalmanalco, Mexico, with its ancient church and pulque magueys. *Photo Franco*

are only two higher plateaus of comparable size in the world: those of Tibet and Bolivia.

The national capital, Mexico City, is a metropolitan center of 20 million people. Its altitude is 7,347 feet. Monterrey, industrial capital of Nuevo León and Mexico's third largest city (estimated at 2.6 million), lies 150 miles south of the Texas border at an altitude of only 1,763 feet, but many of the country's large cities are located at altitudes of more than 5,000 feet. Guadalajara, Jalisco, second largest city, with an estimated 2.8 million population, has an altitude of 5,140 feet.

Two seasons of the year, rather than four, have always been recognized in Mexico: the dry and rainy seasons. Time was when the two seasons were clear-cut and predictable, the rains beginning in May in most of the country and lasting through September. In recent years, however, the seasonal divisions have become blurred, and rain falls frequently in the winter months. The hottest period of the year comes at the end of the dry season, usually from February through April. The central plateau enjoys a year-round mean temperature of 65 degrees.

In Baja California, the northern Pacific Coast area, and the broad heart of the country, from the U. S. border to the central highlands, inadequate rainfall and the resulting scarcity of rivers have always constituted a major problem. In the Gulf Coast region, from Tampico to Campeche, rain falls all year, and in the same area, where they are least needed, are found the most voluminous rivers.

Because so much of its national territory is covered with mountains, and because of insufficient rainfall and the absence of rivers throughout extensive regions, only 19 per cent of Mexico's total land area is even potentially arable. Of the remainder, 48 per cent is devoted to pasture lands on plains and mountainous terrain; 29 per cent is covered with forest; and 4 per cent consists of barren wasteland and swamps.

This, then, is the stage upon which the drama of Mexico's history has been enacted.

THE ANCIENT MEXICANS

Back in the dim and distant days of pre-history, according to the most widely accepted theory, nomadic tribes of Asiatic peoples crossed to this hemisphere by a route not yet determined, and gradually, over a period of centuries, made their way southward through Alaska, Canada, and the United States into what is now the Republic of Mexico. They established no permanent settlements, but lived off the land. They were fishermen, hunters, and gatherers of wild fruits and berries.

On the northern portion of the continent, no architectural or other remains have yet been uncovered to indicate that the early inhabitants of the U. S. and Canada ever advanced beyond the most primitive culture. But at some point in the migration of these nomads over Mexico, a revolutionary change occurred: they discovered wild corn, a plant bearing one small spear of edible grain.

When this fortunate event took place is unknown, but recent explorations over a wide area, from Tamaulipas to Chiapas, indicate the use by man of this early species of corn as long ago as 7,000 to 9,000 years. At that time, the plant's one very small ear, bearing a few tiny grains, was enclosed in a pod, which Nature later replaced with the husk it now wears.

Sometime between the years 5,000 and 3,000 B.C., man succeeded, by a process of selection, in improving that primitive plant, thereby producing corn as we know it, with several large, many-grained ears to the stalk. Certain it is that corn is native to the Americas.

The miracle worked by the discovery of corn was this: wandering tribes of prehistoric peoples became a settled population. Relieved of the necessity to be constantly on the move in search of their daily food, they built houses and settlements, cultivated beans, tomatoes, chile peppers, squash, and other plants, in addition to corn, and had leisure time in which to develop such household crafts as basketmaking, ceramics, and weaving.

Early Civilizations

Long before the birth of Christ, the central and southern regions of Mexico were inhabited by peoples, thought to be descendants of those primitive nomads, who reached a high degree of civilization. First in importance, the Olmecs, from 2000 B.C. to about 200 A.D., lived in an area on the Gulf Coast now covered by the tropical jungles of southern Veracruz and northern Tabasco. They left few architectural remains, because stone is scarce in the vicinity, but they did bequeath to us a wealth of stone sculpture and pottery that reveals not only the extent of their cultural development, but also the fact that they had initiated a numbering system, an almost exact calendar, hieroglyphic writing, and astronomical observations.

Adventuresome as well as creative, the Olmecas colonized many areas, influenced other peoples, and contributed to the formation of several civilizations, notably that of the Teotihuacanos in the central highlands. At Teotihuacan, some 25 miles northeast of Mexico City, stone was abundant and the massive

Pyramids of the Sun and Moon were erected between 100 B.C. and 200 A.D. This enormous city, with an urban area of 8.7 square miles, continued to flourish until 650 A.D., then gradually declined and was finally abandoned 150 years later.

The Teotihuacanos excelled in architecture, mural painting, pottery, and stone sculpture. They were also talented urban planners. As the population increased, new structures were raised, new suburbs added, pushing ever outward from the main ceremonial center. Along the Avenue of the Dead — extending 1.5 miles from the Pyramid of the Moon, past that of the Sun, to the great enclosure known today as the Ciudadela or Citadel — temples, priestly dwellings, palaces, and plazas were built. Beyond them were the homes and workshops of the craftsmen and other ordinary citizens. On the outskirts lived the farmers and laborers. The suburbs were usually composed of blocks of rooms, sometimes as many as 200 joined together, and provided with inner patios, altars, sanitary services, and sewers for the prevention of floods in the rainy season.

Another advanced culture that evidenced Olmec influence developed in southeastern Mexico, in an area that covered the present states of Chiapas and Tabasco, as well as the republics of Guatemala and Honduras, where the Mayas, early in the Christian Era, built the fabulous cities of Palenque and Yaxchilán, among others. Six hundred years later, during the 12th century, Maya civilization reached a new peak, this time in Yucatán, where Chichén Itzá and Uxmal were the principal centers. They had contact with the Caribbean islands and Central America through trading posts such as Cozumel and Tulum.

Apart from their architectural genius, the Mayas achieved remarkable advances along other lines. Even before the Christian Era they had devised a calendar more accurate than the one in use in Europe at that time; it was based on a solar year of 365.242 days.

For many reasons, Maya civilization again declined and reached its nadir about the middle of the 15th century, some 50 years before Columbus set out to reach the Indies by sailing westward.

In Oaxaca, both Mixtecs and Zapotecs left ample evidence of their creative abilities in the monumental architecture of their urban centers, and in the exquisitely worked gold jewelry and other art objects recovered in the course of excavations. In northern Veracruz, and elsewhere, other discoveries have been made of ruins and remains that contribute much to our knowledge of Mexico's ancient inhabitants.

The Aztecs

When Hernán Cortés and his followers first dropped anchor off the coast of Veracruz in April, 1519, just 27 years after the discovery of America, the center of Indian culture and power was the high central plateau. There, in the majestically beautiful Valley of Mexico, Moctezuma II, emperor of the Aztecs, ruled over his own people and exacted tribute from other tribes scattered throughout a vast area of the country.

The Aztecs were relative newcomers, having straggled into the Mexican highlands late in the 13th century. It was not until 1325, just 200 years before the Spanish Conquest, that they founded their capital, Tenochtitlan, now Mexico City, on an island in the largest of the lakes which then filled the valley. There, according to ancient records, they came upon the sign their priests had told them to seek: an eagle, perched on a cactus plant, with a serpent in its beak. History or fable, this is the origin of the national emblem that appears on the Mexican flag and seal.

About the Aztecs we have more information than about any other tribe or nation of ancient Mexicans. This is due to a number of reasons.

First of all, the Spanish conquerors entered Tenochtitlan, a city of approximately 100,000 people, when it was at the height of its glory. They were able, therefore, to observe Aztec civilization with their own eyes, and several of them, notably Bernal Díaz del Castillo, painstakingly recorded their observations.

In the second place, there existed annals, tribal records, in the form of codices. The ancients knew how to make paper from maguey fiber and from the bark of the *amate* tree, a species of fig, as well as parchment from dressed deerskin. On these materials, in vivid colors, they recorded their history by means of a system of picture writing that, by the time of the Conquest, was verging on a written alphabet. In addition to symbols representing numerals, dates, objects, and ideas, they were well advanced in the development of phonetic symbols for syllabic and alphabetical sounds.

Only a few of these precious records escaped destruction immediately after the Conquest: some by Catholic priests and friars who, unable to decipher them, regarded them as instruments of the heathen religion they were determined to uproot; others by chieftains who wished to prevent their tribal records from falling into the hands of the conquerors.

But when Spanish rule had been established, one Franciscan friar, Bernardino de Sahagún, dedicated himself to recording the history of the people as related to him by survivors of the Conquest.

Our third important source of information is the architectural and other remains that continue to be discovered. From them, archaeologists provide us with additional data.

The Aztecs were not the originators, but the developers, of their advanced civilization. When they first appeared on the central plateau they were little better than savages; however, they learned rapidly from the Texcocans, whose capital city was Texcoco on the opposite side of the lake. The Texcocans had absorbed the culture of the Toltecs, who once dominated the Valley of Mexico from their magnificent and populous capital of Tula, in the present state of Hidalgo. And

the Toltecs, in turn, were the direct heirs of the Teotihuacanos.

In November 1519, Hernán Cortés and his men emerged from the pass between the snow-capped peaks of Iztaccihuatl and Popocatepetl to look down upon a sight the like of which they had never seen before.

Stretching immediately beneath them were great forests of pine, oak, and sycamore, giving way on the

Plaza of the Three Cultures, Mexico City, combines the ancient, colonial and modern in striking juxtaposition. Here in Tlatelolco Cuauhtemoc surrendered, here flourished the largest market in America. The pre-Conquest ruins and 16th century church are surrounded by ultramodern housing units.
Photo Franco

lower slopes to cornfields and plantations of maguey that reached to the very shores of the lakes. Nearest them were Lake Chalco and Lake Xochimilco and, beyond, Lake Texcoco. Thousands of canoes, some of them large enough to hold 30 or 40 men, dotted the surface of the lakes.

On an island near the western shore of Lake Texcoco stood the Aztec capital, "the most beautiful city in the world," as Cortés was to describe it to his King.

15

Tenochtitlan covered an area of 2,500 acres, criss-crossed by a geometric network of canals and embankments. Its white towers and temple-crowned pyramids were plainly visible, as were its many stone and adobe houses.

Four causeways — broad enough to permit eight horsemen to ride abreast, Cortés said — connected the island to the mainland. The aqueduct that supplied the city with fresh water from springs near the Hill of Chapultepec, ran northeastward from that point on the western shore to converge with the Tacuba causeway. It was over the causeway from the southeast that the Spaniards first entered the city.

From their lofty vantage point the amazed conquerors could see the great plaza of Tenochtitlan — the Zócalo of today's Mexico City — and, slightly north of it, the tremendous market square of Tlatelolco. To their right, on the eastern shore of the lake, the sun's rays were reflected on the towers and temples of Texcoco. And along the western and southern shores appeared the capital's mainland suburbs.

In two centuries the Aztecs had extended their dominion over a wide area. The "Aztec Empire," as it is commonly referred to, was not an empire in the true sense, for conquered city-states were allowed to retain their own rulers, but warriors captured in battle were carried off to Tenochtitlan to be sacrificed to the gods, and the defeated peoples were required to pay heavy tribute.

At the time of the Conquest, tribute — consisting of foods not produced in the Valley of Mexico, precious stones and metals, feathers of tropical birds, and many other practical and luxury items — was being exacted from subject tribes in the state of Mexico on the west, as far east as Veracruz, and in Puebla, Oaxaca, Morelos, and Guerrero to the south. As an example, the city-state of Tochpan, on the Gulf of Mexico, was required to deliver, each year, 6,948 *cargas,* or loads, of mantles in various sizes, 800 cargas

The Valley of Mexico at the time of the Conquest, 1519.

17

of loincloths and an equal number of skirts; 5,120 bushels of chile peppers; 20 sacks of feathers; two jade necklaces; one turquoise necklace; two turquoise mosaic discs; two suits for Aztec military commanders.

From the beginning, the government that controlled Aztec society was an oligarchy. Several powerful clans supplied leaders to the central government. From among these men was chosen the supreme leader, the *huey tlahtoani* (He Who Speaks with Authority) who, with the passing of time, assumed more and more power until at the time of the Spanish Conquest, Moctezuma II could be presumed to have held almost absolute authority.

The capital city was divided into four sections, each with a number of districts. The districts governed their internal affairs. Ownership of land rested with the community, not with the individual. Since the island population depended largely on nearby sources for its daily food supply, efficient use of the limited amount of land available for cultivation was of primary importance. Each district was assigned an equal portion of tillable land and, in turn, divided it among the heads of families. Possession of the land was continuous, unless a family failed to cultivate it, in which event it was redistributed among more industrious citizens. There is no doubt, however, that food supplied through tribute was vital to the survival of the island population.

In theory, any individual no matter how humble could achieve rank and special privileges for performing some outstanding service to the community as warrior, hunter, farmer or craftsman. However, class distinctions had developed to the extent that the successors of local chieftains were chosen, as a matter of custom, from the same families. Thus, a ruling class had been established. The district officials, together with the military chieftains and high priests, formed what may be regarded as the Aztec nobility.

Not of the nobility, but so influential as a group that they rivaled the nobles in power and prestige, were the merchants, or *pochteca*. Their headquarters were in Tlatelolco, where they occupied seven districts. They were self-governing, electing their own leaders, decreeing their own laws and enforcing them promptly and forcefully. They exercised absolute control over the marketplace of Tlatelolco, the largest and most important market on the American continent. In describing it to the King of Spain, Cortés wrote: ". . . And they have another plaza . . . where more than sixty thousand souls gather daily, buying and selling . . ."

Produce and manufactured goods from as far away as Yucatán, Guatemala, and Honduras were displayed to the astonished gaze of the Spaniards. There were jaguar, puma, fox and deer skins; feathers of eagles, sparrow hawks, falcons, and multicolored tropical birds; corn, beans, chile peppers, cacao and vegetables; medicinal herbs; many kinds of meat, including turkey, rabbit, venison, duck, fattened hairless dogs; dyes for fabrics, paints, cochineal, indigo; vessels of clay; knives and razors of flint or obsidian; reed and clay pipes, tobacco; fish and frogs; jewelry of gold and silver, precious stones; slaves; cotton mantles, skirts, and loincloths.

To secure this colorful assortment of merchandise, caravans set out regularly for distant regions of the country — on foot, with slaves carrying the trade goods, for there were no pack animals in pre-Hispanic Mexico.

Trade was by barter only, in the beginning, and the pochteca carried with them the products of the highlands to exchange, in the tropics, for cacao, jade, lion and tiger skins, quetzal feathers, and many other highly prized articles. Money did not exist, but certain items came to be generally accepted as media of exchange: sacks of cacao beans; goose quills filled with gold dust; small mantles, the size of a handkerchief; sometimes tiny copper axes.

Because their travels took them into alien territory, where they not only learned the language of the people,

The pre-Hispanic Indian system of father-son, mother-daughter apprenticeship has continued in rural areas of modern Mexico. From their mothers, daughters learned craft techniques as well as household duties. Here, in the ethnographic section of the National Museum of Anthropology a girl is shown observing the use of a backstrap loom. *Photo Anne V. Stenzel*

but also had an opportunity to acquaint themselves with the geography, population, military strength, and natural resources of the regions visited, the pochteca became able spies, and were called upon to serve as scouts and advisers in time of war.

Next below the merchants in the Aztec social scale at the beginning of the 16th century were the artisans: painters, masons, carpenters, sculptors, potters, feather workers, jewelers, weavers. Each craftsman worked in his own home, all family members assisting him. His children began at an early age to learn their father's trade.

The great majority of the population belonged to the working class. Each family head was entitled to a plot of land, and his children attended the district schools. He shared in the distribution of food and goods received by the emperor as tribute from subject city-states. As a worker (farmer or artisan) he was exempt from military service; being a warrior was an elite profession and required training in special schools.

The lowest rung on the social ladder was assigned to the slaves, but slavery as practiced in the Aztec

Empire was very different from human bondage elsewhere in the world. No disgrace attached to slavery, the children of slaves were born free, and a slave might marry anyone he chose, even a member of the nobility.

People fell into slavery for a number of reasons. Since the Aztecs did not believe in imprisoning criminals, a thief, for example, would be bound over to the man he had robbed. Prisoners of war who were not immediately sacrificed to the gods served as slaves until the hour of their sacrifice arrived. Some subject city-states were required to furnish a set number of slaves as part of their annual tribute. But the majority were people who voluntarily sold themselves into bondage, to gain freedom from economic worries, because they were too lazy to work the land, or in payment of their own or a relative's debts.

A child's early training was entrusted to its parents. Boys learned to fish, paddle a canoe, and other manly labors, as well as the rudiments of their father's trade, while girls were taught to weave, grind corn for tortillas and, in general, keep house.

But once they reached school age, formal education was compulsory for both sexes. Boys were required to enter one of two types of schools, according to their social status. The *calmecac,* a sort of monastery, was conducted by priests for the sons of nobles, merchants, and a carefully selected few from other social classes. It trained young men for the priesthood and for military and political leadership. Discipline was very strict. Studies included religion — fixing religious feast dates, calculating the calendar, rituals and incantations, how to serve the gods — history, the administration of justice, duties of citizenship, interpretation of picture writing, use of herbs, arithmetic, architecture, astronomy, agriculture, and the art of war.

Most boys attended the *telpochcalli,* or House of Youth, whose purpose was to train young men in citizenship and warfare. In addition, students received

This drawing from the Florentine Codex shows Malintzin, baptized Marina, acting as translator between Cortés and the Aztecs. She was his constant companion throughout the Conquest (1519-21), and rendered invaluable service to the Spaniards. Perhaps with malice, Moctezuma always referred to Cortés as Malinche, and *malinchismo* is a derogatory term that expresses a preference for foreigners or things foreign.

instruction in morals, religion, history, singing, dancing, and the playing of musical instruments.

Similar schools were maintained for girls.

Religion was the moving force in the daily life of every Aztec man, woman and child. Religion drove them to wage war against their neighbors, to study the planets and compute time, to carve idols and build great temples, to offer captives in bloody sacrificial rites on the altars of those temples. The gods they worshiped were many. Some apparently originated with the Aztecs; some were borrowed or adopted from other ancient Mexicans. Religious festivals were governed by the calendar of the Aztec year, which was divided into 18 months of 20 days each, plus five dead days, or days of bad omen. Each month was dedicated to special ceremonies in honor of one of the major deities.

Huitzilopochtli, god of war and of the sun, the young warrior who was born each morning and died again each evening, was the most ancient of Aztec gods, and the one who had guided them into the Valley of Mexico. For his daily battle against the moon and the stars, Huitzilopochtli needed strength. He must be nourished by man, and the only food acceptable to him was human blood.

The Aztecs, as the chosen people of the sun, were charged with the responsibility of providing this food. Waging war for the capture of victims to be sacrificed to the god was, therefore, a form of worship. For this reason the Aztecs were warriors, above all else, and the captives slain were regarded not as enemies but as personal messengers to the god.

Quetzalcoatl, on the other hand, was the wise and humane god of life and of civilization. He taught man agriculture, industry, and the arts. He also taught science, so that man might study the movements of the stars, measure time, and arrange the calendar of the year. Through the trickery of another deity, Quetzalcoatl — frequently shown in the codices as a bearded god — was forced to leave his home in Tula, but promised to return from the east in a year *Ce Acatl* (One Reed).

Since the Aztecs were primarily an agricultural people, gods of water, vegetation, and fertility were numerous and important in their religious life.

Priests in large numbers were required to care for the many temples, supervise the never-ending ceremonies and festivals, and instruct the youth. They exercised total control over education, and were the guardians of all the knowledge and culture possessed by the Aztecs.

When in a year Ce Acatl of the calendar (1519), an exhausted runner brought word to Moctezuma that

23

strange beings, light-skinned and bearded, had appeared off the coast of Veracruz in what seemed to be towers floating on the water, the Aztec Emperor was not taken altogether by surprise.

For 10 years the people had been disturbed by evil omens for which the priests and sorcerers had no satisfactory explanation: a column of fire in the east at midnight every night for an entire year; the temple of Huitzilopochtli consumed by flames; huge comets with fiery tails shooting through the daytime skies; the waters of the lake churned to a frenzy when not even a breeze was blowing; the voice of a woman, wailing in the night.

These and other portents of disaster had weighed heavily on Moctezuma's mind. Now the explanation seemed to be at hand. White, bearded strangers appearing in the east in the year Ce Acatl could mean only one thing: Quetzalcoatl had kept his promise to return.

Comets by day, wailing by night foretold the Conquest.

THE CONQUEST OF MEXICO

The Spanish Conquest, carried out by Hernán Cortés and the forces under his command in the years 1519 to 1521, is one of the most dramatic episodes in Mexico's dramatic history. At first glance, it is difficult to see how it was possible for that small band of adventurers to overthrow the mighty Aztec Empire. Yet all elements combined in favor of the invaders, historians agree.

Cortés himself was fearless and intelligent, a masterful organizer, a natural leader. He and his companions — 110 sailors and 553 soldiers — reached San Juan de Ulúa aboard 11 tiny sailing vessels. Intent on conquering new lands for God and King, Cortés ordered the burning of the ships, thus cutting off all retreat.

The first element in favor of the Spaniards was Moctezuma's belief that they were gods, a belief strengthened by the 16 horses that accompanied them, described by the Indians as 4-legged monsters with human bodies issuing from their backs.

Another was the fact that bows and arrows, darts, lances, stones, and *macanas* — heavy clubs with inset obsidian blades — were no match for the Spaniards' steel armor, knives and swords, muskets, crossbows, and 10 pieces of artillery.

Long-smouldering resentment on the part of tribute-paying city-states enabled Cortés to form alliances with various tribes, who saw the invaders as a spearhead for rebellion.

Communication with tribal leaders all along the route from the sea was made possible by Marina, Cortés' interpreter and constant companion. The daughter of a chieftain and an "excellent woman," according to Bernal Díaz, Marina had been presented to the Conqueror in what is now the state of Tabasco, during his voyage up the Gulf Coast.

The Kingdom of Tlaxcala was the major obstacle in the Spaniards' march from the sea. Sworn enemies of the Aztecs, the Tlaxcalans believed Cortés to be the agent of Moctezuma, and many lives were lost in battle before they could be persuaded that the newcomers wanted only their friendship. Once convinced, the Tlaxcalans became the conquerors' most useful allies.

By this time, through the ambassadors sent repeatedly to confer with Cortés, Moctezuma realized that the unknown white men were not gods but ordinary mortals for, if wounded, they bled and, if wounded severely enough, they died. Nevertheless, each new ambassador brought new, rich gifts to Cortés, together with new arguments against continuing his advance upon the capital.

At last, at the end of a weary march through the pass between Popocatepetl and Iztaccihuatl, the conquerors looked down upon the wonders of Tenochtitlan.

Moctezuma came out to meet them. No resistance was offered to their entrance into the city. They were treated as guests, and housed in the palace of Axayacatl, father of the emperor. Hostility against them did not begin to take definite form until Cortés seized Moctezuma and held him prisoner. Then the people remained in their houses, and the marketplace of

This portrait of Hernán Cortés hangs in the Hospital de Jesús, founded by him in Mexico City where, it is said, Moctezuma first greeted him. Oldest hospital in the Americas, it is still in operation. *Photo INAH*

Tlatelolco was closed, but still no action was taken, despite the tremendous advantage on the side of the Aztecs in sheer force of numbers.

When a messenger brought word from the coast that more Spaniards had arrived under the captaincy of Narváez, Cortés was permitted to leave the city with a small escort. Disaster struck in his absence when the impulsive Pedro de Alvarado, whom he had left in command, fell upon a large gathering of Aztecs celebrating a feast day in a temple and slaughtered them.

Only then did the angry inhabitants rise as one man and drive the Spanish garrison to cover. Cortés, having outwitted Narváez and won over the troops that accompanied him, returned to Tenochtitlan with his reinforcements and was allowed to rejoin the besieged Spaniards, who were kept under continual attack. In the confusion of one Indian assault on the palace-prison, Moctezuma was killed.

After enduring the siege for a week, Cortés decided to withdraw from the city. An hour before dawn on June 30, 1520, the Spaniards began their stealthy retreat over the causeway leading to Tacuba, but were seen by an early riser drawing water from a canal. The alarm was sounded on conch shells and drums, and the attack was on, from rooftops, streets, and canoes.

Soldiers, weighted down with looted treasure, fell into the water and sank. Others were killed outright or captured for immediate sacrifice. Reaching Tacuba, the survivors stopped to tally up their losses. It is said that Cortés, drawing apart from his men, wept bitter tears for most of his companions were slain in the debacle. He then began a roundabout retreat to Tlaxcala. The Texcocans, allies of the Aztecs, attacked the wounded and discouraged Spaniards at Otumba, but turned and fled when their leaders were slain.

In Tlaxcala, Cortés rested his army, won new Indian allies, and conquered nearby towns in preparation for another assault upon the Aztec stronghold.

Meanwhile, Moctezuma had been succeeded by Cuitlahuac. When the latter died of smallpox four months later, 22-year old Cuauhtemoc, nephew and son-in-law of Moctezuma, was elected emperor.

Unlikely as it may seem, it was a naval operation, carried out 7,500 feet above sea level, that played the decisive role in bringing about the downfall of Tenochtitlan.

Ever since his rout from the Aztec capital, Cortés had been devising a novel strategy. In his disorderly flight over the causeway to Tacuba, he had learned well the bitter lesson that Indian archers in canoes could pick off his men at will. A new invasion of the island by way of the causeways alone was unthinkable.

He ordered lumber to be cut in Tlaxcala for 13 brigantines. Indian runners were dispatched to Veracruz to salvage and bring back every fragment of metal, sailcloth, and rigging that remained at the site

The siege of Tenochtitlan lasted 90 days. *Drawing by Alberto Beltrán, after the Florentine Codex*

where he had burned his ships, as well as the cannons abandoned at that time. While this work was under way, Cortés set out for Texcoco, where the brigantines would have to be assembled and launched. There he succeeded in convincing the Texcocans that they had nothing to gain by continued opposition to the Spaniards.

When everything was in readiness, a crew of 8,000 bearers transported timber and fittings across the mountains from Tlaxcala to Texcoco. By the end of April 1521, construction of the warships was completed, and a formidable fleet of war canoes mobilized.

Then Cortés reviewed his troops, counting 928 Spaniards: 84 horsemen, 650 soldiers armed with swords and shields, 194 crossbowmen and musketeers. He chose to take personal command of the naval force and, after manning all vessels and installing the cannons aboard the brigantines, he divided the remainder of his soldiery into three armies, assigning to each a portion of the countless thousands of Indian warriors he had rallied to his banner. The assault began simultaneously over the causeways from Coyoacán and Ixtapalapa on the south and southeast, from Tacuba on the west, and by water from Texcoco on the east.

Outnumbered and outmaneuvered, their food and drinking water supplies from the mainland cut off, and their ranks decimated by smallpox and other diseases introduced by the Spaniards, the valiant Aztecs nevertheless withstood a 90-day siege, capitulating only upon the capture of Cuauhtemoc on August 13, 1521.

Monumental baroque churches like this one dedicated to La Virgen de la Soledad (Virgin of Solitude) in the city of Oaxaca were built throughout Mexico during the colonial period. *Photo Enrique Franco Torrijos*

THE COLONIAL ERA

The fall of once proud and lovely Tenochtitlan gave the Spaniards possession of the central provinces of Mexico. Cortés, an able administrator as well as conqueror, began immediately to rebuild the city, requested the King of Spain to send friars to Christianize the inhabitants, and dispatched his lieutenants to the east, west and south to conquer new tribes, explore the territory, and discover, if possible, the sea route to Asia of which the Spaniards still dreamed.

In the next few years his expeditions had covered the country, from the Gulf of California (also known as the Sea of Cortés) to Guatemala, Yucatán, and

Honduras. It was on the march to Honduras, late in 1524, that Cortés ordered Cuauhtemoc, whom he still held prisoner, to be hung on suspicion of inciting revolt among the Indian allies who accompanied him.

In the meantime, enemies of Cortés, envious of the glory he had won, were busy planting doubts in the mind of the Spanish monarch, accusing the Conqueror of planning to establish an independent kingdom. An *audiencia,* a court of investigation with executive powers, was sent to govern New Spain, as Mexico was then called, and to hear charges against Cortés. Badgered on all sides, he finally set sail for Spain, early in 1528, to present his case personally to the Crown.

Cortés succeeded in making his peace with the King, who bestowed upon him the title of Marquis of the Valley of Oaxaca, and a vast estate including the Valley of Toluca, the province of Cuernavaca, Coyoacán, part of the state of Veracruz, a large portion of the Valley of Oaxaca, and the Isthmus of Tehuantepec — some 25,000 square miles. But rule Mexico he could not.

Refused entrance into Mexico City upon his return in 1530, Cortés retired to Cuernavaca, where he built his palace and worked untiringly for the progress of his adopted country. But his enemies continued to attack him until, nine years later, he returned again to Spain. Ignored by the monarch, he died there in 1547, bitter and disillusioned.

The second audiencia, composed of capable, intelligent men, ruled New Spain from 1530 to 1535, when it became a Viceroyalty and Antonio de Mendoza was named first Viceroy (literally, deputy king). Viceroys — 61 of them — were to govern Mexico until 1821.

It was during the 15 years of Mendoza's rule that Spanish adventurers, in pursuit of mythical treasures and cities of gold, explored not only the whole northern region of what is now the Republic of Mexico, but also an extensive area of what was to become the United States of America, claiming the territory for

Spain. Their names and daring exploits belong equally to the history of both countries: Ponce de León and Pánfilo de Narváez in Florida; Cabeza de Vaca in Texas and New Mexico; Hernando de Soto in the territory lying between the Atlantic Ocean and the Mississippi River; Coronado, as far north as Kansas. All this took place some 80 years before the Pilgrims landed on Plymouth Rock.

Spain's official policy with regard to its colonies was, on the whole, a humane one. True, the colonies were expected to provide the mother country with the funds necessary to finance the endless wars that Spanish kings were to wage all over Europe for more than two centuries. Aside from that, Spanish culture was to be impressed upon the New World, and the Indians were to be converted, educated, and protected.

But in practice the Crown was too far removed from the scene to enforce the laws enacted. The Viceroys found it expedient to govern New Spain in accordance with the realities of the situation.

Caste System

After the first generation, Mexico's inhabitants were divided into well-defined castes. At the top were the Spaniards born in Spain, or *gachupines,* who controlled the political as well as the spiritual life of the country. All government officials, from the Viceroy down to local tax collectors, were Spaniards.

The conquered territory was divided economically, groups of inhabitants being "commended" (*encomiendas*) to Spaniards to use as a work force. Beginning with the conquerors, more than 500 Spaniards were granted encomiendas; other Indian groups were retained by the King in royal encomiendas.

In return for converting the natives, educating and protecting them, the *encomendero* was entitled to their unpaid labor in his fields or mines. Some honest men carried out their obligations to the Indians in their charge. The great majority ignored them. Title to the

33

This 18th century palace, noted for its rich stone and wood carving, was home to the Counts of Santiago de Calimaya, wealthy hacendados. Completely restored in 1960, it houses the Museum of the City of Mexico. *Photo José Luis Neyra*

land, in theory, rested with the Spanish Crown, but in time ownership by the descendants of the original encomenderos was recognized.

Children of Spaniards, born in Mexico of pure Spanish blood, were known as Creoles. Denied the right to hold posts in either the government or the higher ranks of the clergy, they lived for the most part in idleness in Mexico City, supported in luxury by the labor of their Indians — whom they left to the tender mercies of overseers on distant encomiendas and mining properties.

The third, despised sector of the population consisted of the mestizos, those of mixed Spanish and Indian blood. Unlike the English and Dutch settlers who were to colonize the eastern seaboard of the United States, the Spanish conquerors brought no women with them —except for the 12 mentioned below. The families of some later joined them in Mexico and, as the country was gradually pacified, more family groups arrived. But the scarcity of Spanish women led to the union of Spaniards with Indian women, and to the birth of many children of mixed blood.

The mestizos, whose number increased daily, and who now account for 75 to 80 per cent of the country's total population, were regarded as outcasts until late in the Colonial Era.

Most numerous, of course, were the Indians who, in the beginning and despite Spanish laws for their protection, were scarcely looked upon as human beings at all. It has been estimated that, at the time of the Conquest, there were about nine million Indians on Mexico's central plateau. By 1600 their number did not exceed 2.5 million.

Many fled after the coming of the Spaniards, establishing themselves in isolated mountain valleys. Hundreds of thousands died during the years immediately following the Conquest, victims of the diseases brought in by the newcomers: tuberculosis, smallpox, measles, the plague, and the common cold. Other hundreds of thousands were literally worked to death in the fields, in the mines, and taking the place of pack animals for, until after the Conquest, man was the only beast of burden. In addition to horses, the Spaniards introduced burros, mules, and oxen, as well as sheep, goats, chickens, cattle, and house pets. But it took a number of years to breed sufficient draft animals to relieve the Indians of their back-breaking labor.

At the bottom of the social caste system, beginning less than 20 years after the Conquest, were the black

slaves, brought in from Africa to work on the sugar-cane plantations, in the mines and mills.

It was Mexican anthropologist Dr. Gonzalo Aguirre Beltrán who, in 1946, first focused attention on the volume and importance of black immigration during the Colonial Era, basing his research on official and religious archives, including material in Inquisition documents that had until then escaped the notice of historians and ethnographers. His work revealed a surprising chapter in Mexican history.

The first blacks, Christianized in Spain, arrived with the conquerors in 1519, as personal servants. Smallpox, which took such a heavy toll among the Indians, was introduced by one of them. Another brought in and planted the first grains of wheat, a foodstuff that, in time and within certain areas, was to modify the traditional diet of the people. Of the 12 women who accompanied the Spaniards, three were mulattoes.

By 1540 a triangular trade route was well establish-ed. Sailing vessels, many of them English, transported European manufactured goods from Spain to West African ports. There they took on a cargo of blacks, to be sold into slavery in Mexico. Then they returned to Spain laden with sugar, leather, cochineal, cacao, and other coveted New World products. This three-cornered voyage was repeated time after time.

Familiar figures on the streets of the colonial capital were the night watchman and the public scribe, facing page, and *pregoneros* like the candle vendor. House-to-house salesmen of water, flowers, fish, meat, and all other staples had their distinctive *pregones*, or cries.

According to contracts still in existence, entered into between Spanish monarchs and the slave traders, at least 250,000 blacks, one-third of them women, were brought into Mexico during the Colonial Period, most of them before 1640. The significance of this immigration figure is underlined by the fact that, during the three centuries of Spanish domination, fewer than 200,000 Spaniards and other Europeans entered Mexico, whether to settle or merely passing through. Of that total, only 10 per cent were women. At any given time, the number of Europeans living in New Spain was extremely small: a census taken in 1793, by order of Viceroy Revillagigedo, showed 7,904 European residents in the entire country.

Serfdom for those Indians who failed to escape from the Spanish sphere of influence — into remote jungle and mountain areas where, without interference, they could continue their communal way of life and tribal form of government — persisted until they were liberated by the Revolution of 1910. But slavery began to disappear a century earlier, when plantation, mine and factory owners came to realize that paid labor was much cheaper. Slavery was abolished altogether in the mid-1800's.

Meanwhile, the blacks were almost completely absorbed into the population, in a heterogeneous array of mixtures, resulting from their union with Spaniards,

Indians, mestizos, and mulattoes that defied classification by colonial authorities. Black heritage is most clearly evident in the states of Veracruz, Puebla, Oaxaca, Tabasco, Morelos and Guerrero, and still predominates in a few isolated villages.

Apparently the black's vital role in Mexico's economic development became obscured due to the fact that scientific study and research on the part of historians and anthropologists was not undertaken until around 1910. By then the blacks had disappeared as a readily identifiable group. It was the Indian and all his needs and attributes that claimed the attention of post-Revolutionary writers, educators, muralists, and politicians.

Role of the Church

Conversion of the Indians began in earnest in 1524 with the arrival of the first group of Franciscan missionary friars. After them came the Dominicans, the Augustinians, and the Jesuits.

Armed with nothing more than faith and good will, these early missionaries set about the spiritual conquest of New Spain in a manner as daring and energetic as that of the Great Conqueror himself. Some established schools for the sons of Indian nobles in Texcoco, Tlatelolco, and elsewhere in the more populous areas near the capital. Others built missions in remote small towns and rural areas. They studied the various Indian languages, taught the fundamentals of the Christian doctrine, and performed the ceremonies of baptism, marriage, and burial, as well as regular masses. In addition, they made friends with the Indians by teaching them European methods of weaving, dyeing, masonry, ceramics, and agriculture.

Some of these dedicated men left a vivid and indelible imprint on the pages of Mexican history. Among them are Pedro de Gante, Bernardino de Sahagún, Vasco de Quiroga, and Toribio de Benavente, more generally known as Motolinía.

The 16th century churches and convents that adorn the Mexican landscape today were built by Indians, under the direction of missionary friars. One wonders how, with the primitive tools and techniques at their disposal, it was possible to create the architectural gems that continue to be one of Mexico's great artistic assets. At least 100,000 religious buildings were constructed during the Colonial Era.

In order to understand the role of the Catholic Church in Mexico it is necessary to bear in mind two facts. First, when Queen Isabela of Spain, just before the discovery of America, succeeded in ousting the Moors from Granada, she demanded, and received, from the Pope the right to nominate men for all offices in the Spanish church. This meant that every member of the Catholic clergy in Spain was a salaried employee of the Crown. It also meant complete identification of Church with Government.

The second point to be remembered is that only the secular, or regular, clergy was included under the Papal grant of power to the Spanish Crown. The missionary orders, on the other hand, in a decree issued by Pope Leo X in 1521, were declared to be self-governing bodies with extraordinary powers, and no secular priest might interfere with them, on penalty of excommunication.

In Mexico, therefore, from the days of the first Viceroy, Church and State worked hand in hand when, indeed, they were not one and the same thing: several of the Viceroys were also high churchmen. The missionary friars carried on their labors independently, exerting far more influence over the people than the secular clergy, until 1640.

King Silver

Although the conquerors failed to find immediately the treasures their imagination had led them to expect, treasure was nevertheless forthcoming later upon the discovery of gold and silver mines, which produced riches beyond their wildest dreams.

Silver was king in Mexico from 1570 to 1821. In only 350 years mines in the states of Hidalgo, Guanajuato, Zacatecas, Durango, and Guerrero doubled the world's silver supply.

One-fifth of all silver mined belonged to the Spanish Crown, but much of it never reached Spain. That was the age of piracy, and bold English and Dutch buccaneers won handsome rewards and even titles of nobility for preying upon treasure-laden Spanish galleons. For 200 years the exploits of Hawkins and Frobisher, Raleigh and Drake, Thomas Cavendish,

Old engraving shows Acapulco and first San Diego Fort in 17th century. Built to protect shipping from attack by pirates. the Fort's chief concern was the safety of famed *Nao de China* on her annual arrival from the Philippines with priceless cargo. Fort in center marked "B" and Puerto Marqués, "F"
Photo Franco

Lorenzo de Graaf, and other equally celebrated pirates made them heroes at home and demons in the minds of Spanish sailors and the inhabitants of Mexican ports. Theirs was a "share the wealth" campaign that enriched all of Europe.

Prelude to Revolt

By 1800, education, completely dominated by the Church, had long since become the exclusive property of the privileged classes. Besides the University in Mexico City, founded in 1551, some 40 colleges and

41

seminaries were in operation, training students for the priesthood and for entrance into the University.

At the beginning of the 19th century, conditions within Mexico and events in other parts of the world combined to make revolt against Spain inevitable.

The encomienda system, with its doubtful safeguards for the Indians, had finally been abolished, only to be replaced by the hacienda system, under which they were reduced to virtual slavery. Many of the *ejidos,* agricultural lands worked communally by the Indians since time immemorial, by 1800 were absorbed into the great haciendas.

Largest landowner of all was the Catholic Church. At the close of the Colonial Era, it owned more than half of the land and buildings in Mexico, through gifts, bequests, and mortgages. Since church property was exempt from taxation, half the country's real wealth, therefore, was producing no income for the national treasury.

Resentment on the part of wealthy Creoles against the gachupines who governed them, and against Spain's economic policy, which prohibited Mexico from trading with any other country, had reached the boiling point.

Culturally and politically, Mexico was as isolated as the Spanish kings and the Holy Inquisition could keep it. Due to the fact that Spain carefully screened newcomers to the colony, the Inquisition in Mexico had few heretics with whom to deal. Its efforts were devoted chiefly to censorship of reading material in an attempt to prevent the spread of dangerous ideas during that unsettled period in world history.

In 1776, the American Revolution set an example for all European colonies in the Western Hemisphere. Of even greater influence was the French Revolution that followed shortly thereafter. Writings of Rousseau and other revolutionaries were smuggled into Mexico and eagerly read in meetings of the dozens of secret societies that sprang up.

Benito Juárez, Miguel Hidalgo, and José María Morelos, as portrayed by Diego Rivera in his mosaic mural on the facade of the Teatro Insurgentes in Mexico City. *Photo Anne V. Stenzel*

INDEPENDENT MEXICO, 1810-1910

War for Independence

Miguel Hidalgo y Costilla was the parish priest in the village of Dolores, Guanajuato. A Creole prevented from rising to a higher position in the Church, he became an active member of the Literary and Social Club of Querétaro, a secret society led by another Creole, Captain Ignacio Allende, commander of a local militia. In sessions of this group a plot was hatched: on December 8, 1810, the armed forces under Allende were to proclaim Mexico's independence from Spain.

News of the conspiracy leaked out to Spanish authorities. Allende was warned and immediately set out to alert Hidalgo in Dolores. The parish priest decided that the blow for freedom must be struck then and there.

At some time during that night of September 15-16, 1810, Hidalgo rang the church bell to call the villagers together. When they were gathered around him, he raised his voice in the first *Grito de Dolores*, a cry that is repeated each year at 11 p.m. on September 15, the eve of Mexico's Independence Day, by the President of the Republic and by state governors and mayors in every city and town.

"Long live Our Lady of Guadalupe!" he cried. "Death to bad government!" And his listeners responded: "Death to the Spaniards!"

Hidalgo was not a military man, and no advance preparations had been made to arm, or even to feed, the mob of 50,000 Indians, mestizos, mulattoes, and Creoles attracted to his banner by the end of the first week. Without military training, their weapons, with few exceptions, consisting of machetes, daggers, slingshots, clubs, and crude spears, they swept through the countryside, burning, looting, and gathering recruits. On November 2, they won their greatest victory at Las Cruces, in the state of Mexico.

Toward the end of the year, Hidalgo and Allende led their forces into Guadalajara. There Allende ordered the casting of cannons and the manufacture of ammunition, and tried to organize his 80,000 men, who until then had fought mainly on frenzied enthusiasm, into an army. But it was too late. On January 17, 1811, the rebel forces were attacked and badly beaten by 6,000 disciplined troops under the Spanish General Calleja.

44

Hidalgo and his military staff fled northward to Saltillo, where they were captured a month later. After a march to Chihuahua, across 200 miles of desert, Hidalgo, Allende, and other rebel officers were executed as traitors.

In the wilds of Guerrero another priest, José María Morelos, a mestizo, was heading the independence movement in the south. As a political planner and military strategist, Morelos was a far more able man than Hidalgo. Whereas Hidalgo's campaign had been based on emotion and hatred of the Spaniards, Morelos planned with cold logic. He was the first to define the goals of the revolution.

During a congress called by him at Chilpancingo in November 1813, Morelos outlined his program. Mexico was to be totally independent from Spain. None but the Catholic religion was to be permitted, but the Church must thenceforth live exclusively from tithes. The people were to be governed by their own elected representatives. No foreigner might hold a government office, and no foreigners, except skilled mechanics free of political ties, might remain in the country. Slavery and class distinctions were abolished. All Mexicans were to be equal under the law. The right to possess property was held sacred, and a man's house was declared to be his castle. Government monopolies, sales taxes, and tributes were abolished, and the Republic was to be financed through taxes on income and duties on imports of foreign goods.

But after five years of brilliant military campaigning Morelos was captured by Spanish forces and brought to Mexico City, where he was defrocked by the Holy Office. On December 22, 1815, he met his death before a firing squad.

Independence from Spain did not come until September 27, 1821, when Colonel Agustín Iturbide took the capital. By that time, those who set the insurrection in motion had been nearly forgotten, and the

HISTORICAL MAP OF
MEXICO

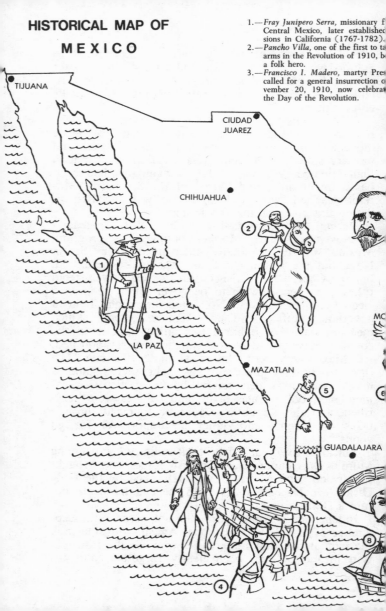

1.— *Fray Junipero Serra*, missionary f
Central Mexico, later established
sions in California (1767-1782).
2.— *Pancho Villa*, one of the first to ta
arms in the Revolution of 1910, b
a folk hero.
3.— *Francisco I. Madero*, martyr Pres
called for a general insurrection o
vember 20, 1910, now celebra
the Day of the Revolution.

TIJUANA

CIUDAD
JUAREZ

CHIHUAHUA

LA PAZ

MAZATLAN

GUADALAJARA

MO

4.—*Maximilian*, whose shortlived empire lasted only three years (1864-67), was executed with his generals in Querétaro.

5.—*Don Vasco de Quiroga* (1470-1565), beloved Bishop of Michoacán, built hospitals and restructured the Indians in ancient crafts.

6.—*Miguel Hidalgo* proclaimed independence from Spain on the night of September 15-16, 1810, and launched the revolt that finally succeeded 10 years later.

7.—*Porfirio Díaz*, first a war hero, held the presidency as a dictator for 35 years (1876-1911).

8.—*Nao de la China*. The galleon that carried profitable trade items yearly over the route Acapulco-Phillipines was so designated. This commerce — silver from New Spain, silks and spices from the Orient, lasted nearly 250 years.

9.—*Emiliano Zapata*, agrarian leader of the Revolution of 1910, recruited armies of villagers in the state of Morelos.

10.—*In the Valley of Mexico*, ancient cultures reached high levels of civilization: the Teotihuacano, Toltec, and Aztec.

11.—*The city of Puebla* was founded in 1531, a Spanish city without an Indian heritage. Its imposing Cathedral bespeaks its religious and economic importance in New Spain.

12.—*Hernán Cortés* led his army from Veracruz to the high Valley of Mexico where he conquered Tenochtitlan, the Aztec capital, in 1521.

13.—*Benito Juárez*, Mexico's Reform President, led the nation through a very difficult period — the French intervention, and the War of Reform which drastically curbed the Catholic Church's power.

14.—*Caravelle*. These fast light vessels communicated Spain and her new American colonies in the 16th century.

15.—*The Arch of Labná* in southern Yucatán is one of many gems of Maya arquitecture.

16.—*Palenque*. This Maya site on the westernmost edge of the Maya area is considered perhaps the most beautiful of all. Here sculpture reached supreme excellence in execution and inspiration.

17.—*The gorgeous Quetzal bird*, still found in the Chiapas highlands, was an important symbol in the ancient Maya religion.

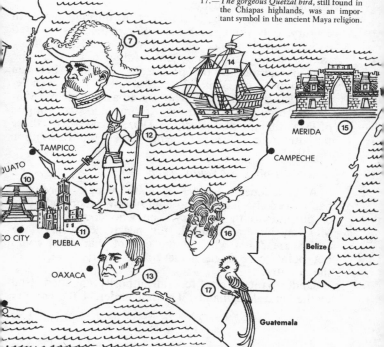

ideals that motivated them had been modified. Political viewpoints changed with the result that independence was finally achieved by a combination of Spanish officials, conservative Creoles, and most of the higher clergy.

Mexico was in chaos. All production was at a standstill. No native-born Mexican had any experience in government. And a new class—the military—had come into existence. Generals, either in the presidency or behind the scenes, were to control the country's destiny almost without interruption for 100 years.

Between 1822, when Iturbide proclaimed himself emperor — his "empire" lasted a mere 10 months — and 1876, when Porfirio Díaz established a dictatorship that was to be prolonged for 35 years, Mexico had two emperors, 40 presidents, and a number of provisional governments.

Of all those who held control during the 19th century, only three, each for different reasons, exerted a significant influence on the history of Mexico. They were Antonio López de Santa Anna, a Creole, who was in and out of the presidency 11 times between 1832 and 1855; Benito Juárez, a full-blooded Zapoteca Indian from Oaxaca, who served as president 1858-1872, through the War of Reform and the Empire of Maximilian; and Porfirio Díaz, a mestizo, whose despotic rule, 1876-1911, engendered the Revolution of 1910.

Antonio López de Santa Anna

After independence was won, the people of Mexico badly needed a leader who could bring order and unity of purpose to the country, one who could mold the Mexican Nation. Instead, for nearly 25 years they had Santa Anna who, at the end of that time, could not point to a single achievement for the welfare of the country.

Under Santa Anna, federal authority confined itself to the central highlands. The remainder of the country fell into the hands of local strong men, who set up their own private kingdoms. Payrolls of the military kept the national treasury in a constant state of bankruptcy.

But Santa Anna has gone down in history chiefly because of the loss of territory Mexico suffered under his various administrations.

First, Mexican and American settlers in the Mexican province of Texas succeeded in winning their independence in 1836, after soundly defeating Santa Anna in the Battle of San Jacinto. Nine years later, when the Republic of Texas became the 28th state in the United States, war broke out again and U. S. troops invaded Mexico: from the north under Zachary Taylor, from the Gulf Coast under Winfield Scott.

Once more Santa Anna was recalled from exile to recruit an army. In his customary flamboyant style, he lost several major engagements on both fronts but contrived to sell them as victories to the general public, thanks to the nonexistence of rapid communications. Scott's forces occupied Mexico City on September 13, 1847.

By the Treaty of Guadalupe Hidalgo, signed several months after the war ended, the Mexican territories of Arizona, New Mexico, and California, in addition to Texas, were ceded to the United States. Santa Anna could claim the distinction of having lost for Mexico half its national territory.

Benito Juárez

Juárez, the first real leader of Mexican liberals, was Santa Anna's opposite in every respect.

Born of humble Indian parents in Oaxaca, he was taken to the state capital at an early age by a protector who wished to educate him for the priesthood. After several years in a seminary, however, Juárez realized he had no aptitude for the priesthood. He took up the study of law instead, a field in which he excelled. After serving terms in both the state legislature of

Oaxaca and the national Congress, he was elected governor of Oaxaca. When Comonfort became president after Santa Anna's final exit from the scene, Juárez was named to head the Ministry of Justice.

A stern, unsmiling man, Juárez was deeply religious, wholly dedicated to the cause of justice under the law. In their personal history, as well as in the nature and the strength of their convictions, he and his contemporary, Abraham Lincoln, had much in common.

From illiterate shepherd to president of his country at the time of its greatest peril was the path trod by Benito Juárez. The historian Parkes says he displayed a moral grandeur unequaled in Mexico's history. A liberal and a Mason from his student days, he preserved the nation during civil war and foreign invasion. *Photo Casasola*

Born in 1806, Juárez spent his childhood herding sheep. Lincoln first saw the light of day in 1809, on a poverty stricken Kentucky farm. Both men were liberals, though the causes they espoused were different, and each was to alter drastically the course of his country's history.

The two never met, but they exchanged correspondence during Lincoln's term of office, 1861-65. When news of the latter's assassination reached him, Juárez mourned the loss of a friend and kindred spirit.

By an odd trick of fate, when the mestizos at last came into their own, it was under the leadership of a full-blooded Indian. Most of the Creoles clung to the old, conservative order of things, although the liberals among them supported Juárez.

At that time, the term "liberal" meant anti-clerical, and "conservative," pro-clerical. The Catholic Church had become the main issue. Yet the attack on the Church was not an attack on religion. Its objective was to curb the economic and political power of the Church, which was stunting the nation.

Adoption of the liberal Constitution of 1857 brought this all-important issue to a head. Among other things, it abolished special-privilege courts for members of the clergy and army officers, directed that church lands be confiscated and sold, provided for government schools, and authorized civil marriages.

This marked the beginning of open warfare between Church and State. The War of Reform, as it was called, lasted for three years, until 1860. At its outbreak, Comonfort was forced to resign. Benito Juárez, proclaimed constitutional president of a government that was obliged to flee the capital, directed the liberal forces from Veracruz, where in 1859 he published laws implementing the 1857 Constitution.

Conservative forces won most of the battles, but they could not win the war, for the liberals fought in guerrilla bands that melted into the hills. On New Year's Day, 1861, the liberals made their triumphal entry into Mexico City. Conservative leaders withdrew to the provinces and plotted to set up a monarchy by bringing into the country a European prince.

Juárez needed all his courage to face the problems that awaited him. The national treasury was bankrupt, and 80 million pesos in loans and debts of various kinds were long overdue. England, Spain, and France were Mexico's chief creditors.

Napoleon III, Emperor of France, entered into an agreement with England and Spain for collection of the money owing to them. According to its terms, naval forces of the three nations were merely to occupy Mexican ports until the debts were paid.

But without the knowledge of his co-signers, Napoleon, convinced by conservative agents in Europe that the Mexicans would welcome a strong foreign ruler, had persuaded the young Archduke Maximilian of Austria to accept the throne of Mexico. Emperor Maximilian was to be supported for three years by a French army of occupation.

The fact that the Civil War had just begun in the United States gave Napoleon reason to believe there would be no interference from that quarter.

As soon as Spain and England recognized Napoleon's true purpose, they canceled their agreement with him. On January 7, 1862, French warships dropped anchor in the port of Veracruz and French troops began their march on the capital.

Again the country was plunged into war. Again Benito Juárez took to the famous black coach which had served as headquarters of the constitutional government during the War of Reform.

The liberals gained one glorious victory, on May 5, 1862, when forces under the command of Ignacio Zaragoza routed the French army at Puebla. But after that, the invaders had little difficulty in taking the capital. French reinforcements continued to arrive, and the liberals sought sanctuary in the mountains as they had done before. Finally, Napoleon felt that the country was sufficiently subdued to receive its new master.

Maximilian and his wife, Carlota, landed in Veracruz on May 28, 1864. Although the French had not been long in discovering that the Mexican conservatives had tricked them, Maximilian was left in ignorance of the true state of affairs. An idealist and an honorable man, he came to accept a throne which, in all good faith, he believed was being offered to him by the Mexican people. But for Mexicans, Maximilian was an alien intruder and they would have none of him. At this distance, a century later, the entire episode seems like a fantastic fairy tale; one that, from the beginning, was destined to end in tragedy.

Juárez, riding through the back country in his black carriage, held the liberals together and gained recruits; for the French invasion accomplished what nothing else had been able to bring about: it welded the people of Mexico into a nation.

Meanwhile, the Civil War in the U. S. came to an end. Napoleon, threatened by Prussia, needed his soldiers at home. Furthermore, the U. S. government was suggesting to him that French troops were unwelcome in the Western Hemisphere.

When Maximilian could not be persuaded to abdicate, he was left behind. Carlota, who had returned to Europe to seek aid for her husband, went insane and was confined to a castle in Belgium, where she remained until her death in 1927. On June 19, 1867, Maximilian faced a firing squad on the Cerro de las Campanas (Hill of the Bells) in Querétaro.

That same year, Juárez was elected to his third term as president. Realizing that militarism was the greatest threat to a democratic government, he dismissed 40,000 officers and men from the army. Outraged generals revolted and were promptly crushed. Porfirio Díaz, one of the ablest of those who had fought for the liberal cause, resentful of what he considered rank ingratitude on the part of Juárez, retired to his hacienda in Oaxaca to bide his time.

Determined to institute orderly government, Juárez attempted to reduce the national debt. Industry and commerce, even though mainly in the hands of foreigners, began to grow. The railroad from Veracruz to Mexico City, started in 1850, was finally completed. Thousands of schools were built; but so great was the need, by 1874 primary education was still available to only one of seven school-age children.

In 1871 Juárez ran for a fourth term. He was opposed by both Porfirio Díaz and Sebastián Lerdo de Tejada. No one of the three received a majority of the votes, and the election was thrown into Congress. Juárez was chosen president, Lerdo was named to head the Supreme Court, and Díaz revolted, but was soundly defeated in the field.

The following year, on July 18, 1872, Benito Juárez, the man who had really governed Mexico for the first time in its history, died of a heart attack. His guiding principle in domestic and foreign relations, "Respect for the rights of others means peace," is as valid today as it was 100 years ago.

Lerdo de Tejada succeeded Juárez in the presidency, but when he announced, in 1876, that he would seek a second term, Díaz declared against him, adopting as his slogan "Effective Suffrage, No Re-election." Lerdo was defeated and forced into exile. Porfirio Díaz assumed the presidency on November 21, 1876, a post he was to hold, except for one 4-year term, until May 24, 1911.

Porfirio Díaz

Porfirio Díaz, the most efficient despot Latin America has ever produced, was an uneducated man, a politician by nature, a clever and ruthless ruler. A professed liberal, he soon aligned himself with the conservatives.

From the material standpoint, Mexico made phenomenal progress under his administration. Whereas Juárez had been equally concerned with the creation of a democratic government and the economic development of the country, Díaz sacrificed the first goal in favor of the second.

As an initial step, order was imposed. The dictator's distrust of the military was as great as Juárez' had been; but instead of discharging generals and soldiers, he split them up into small contingents, sent them to staff unimportant garrisons all over the country, and left them to rot. Provincial strong men who had helped put him in power were either placed

Exhibiting the many medals bestowed upon him by foreign governments, dictator Porfirio Díaz, right, appears here with U.S. Ambassador Henry Lane Wilson who, a few years later, was to connive with a usurper. *Photo Casasola*

on the government payroll or held in check by the granting of favors of another kind.

To deal with bandits who infested the hills, strikers, protesting Indians, and other troublesome sectors of the population, Díaz created a private police force, known as the *Rurales,* recruiting its members from among city thugs and the bandits themselves. These political police were well paid, provided with handsome uniforms, and authorized to shoot on sight.

Church lands confiscated under the Reform Laws had long since been acquired by private citizens, but

Díaz ignored such laws as he chose, and the Church was allowed to function as it had in the past.

With the country at peace, foreign investors were encouraged to work the long-neglected mines, to exploit the rich oil deposits, refine sugar, and build some 8,000 factories.

As a result, the 578 kilometers of railroad track laid by 1876 increased to 19.9 thousand kilometers by 1910. Foreign trade swelled from 51.8 million pesos to 10 times that amount in the same period. A single bank existed in 1876, with capital and assets of 2.5 million pesos, but by 1910 there were 32 banks with capital and assets of 764 million pesos. Federal income rose from 19.8 to 111 million pesos.

Although it is to Díaz that credit is usually given for the prodigious growth of Mexico's economy during the last 16 years of his reign, the financial genius in fact responsible for that growth was José Ivés Limantour, Minister of the Treasury 1893-1911. Born in Mexico City in 1854, the illegitimate son of a French adventurer, he chose Mexican citizenship in 1875.

The national treasury was not only bankrupt but hopelessly in debt when Díaz went into office, and little headway toward rectifying that situation had been made by 1893. Limantour energetically set to work, marshaled the nation's resources, paid off its debts and, in the fiscal year 1894-95, gave Mexico the first surplus it had enjoyed in all its history: 19,681 pesos. By 1910, he had amassed a surplus of 136 million pesos.

As advisers, Limantour gathered around him a group of brilliant young lawyers, economists and intellectuals, members of the generation that had grown to maturity after the Reform Era. Never more than 16 in number, they became known as the *científicos* because of their advocacy of honesty and scientific expertise in the handling of governmental affairs. They were all Creoles, however — the sons of Europeans who arrived in Mexico after independence was achieved — and regarded Indians and mestizos with utter disdain. As a result, the lot of those two sectors of the population steadily worsened, whereas the country's economic position steadily improved due, in large part, to the greatly increased foreign investments made with the encouragement and advice of the científicos.

In the eyes of the world — and of perhaps, one-fourth of the Mexicans — the country had at last attained political and economic stability. The dictator himself was praised at home and abroad as an enlightened ruler, the savior of Mexico.

But apart from the industries established and controlled almost entirely by foreigners, Mexico and Mexicans had reverted to a feudal agricultural society, based on a greatly expanded hacienda system. As one writer has expressed it, two civilizations lived side by side in the Mexico of Porfirio Díaz: the 20th century of the wealthy, cultivated minority, and the 12th century of early medieval serfs, the latter including at least 75 per cent of the population.

Between 1883 and 1894 Díaz gave away, at nine cents per acre, to land speculators and personal friends, 134.5 million acres of public lands. That accomplished, he next ordered the breaking up of lands until then, and for centuries past, worked communally by the Indians and authorized their distribution as private property.

By 1910, 85 per cent of the rural population was landless, and less than 1,000 families owned 90 per cent of the land of Mexico. There were 8,245 haciendas, many of them enormous. Largest of them all, the Terrazas estate in Chihuahua embraced 33.7 million acres, an area equal to that of Arkansas. Each hacienda was a kingdom unto itself, and almost completely self-sufficient.

The great bulk of the rural population was converted into peons, agricultural slaves, who toiled long hours for a theoretical wage of 120 pesos per year. As a matter of fact, the peon never held currency in his hand — except when, in case of funerals or marriages, he was forced to borrow money from the *hacendado,* the hacienda owner — for all the necessities of his miserable life were secured, on credit, from the hacienda store. Thus, he was always in debt to the hacendado and, upon dying, his debts were the legacy he passed on to his children.

Agricultural methods were of the most primitive, for manpower was cheap and abundant and machinery was costly. Therefore, the hacienda system gave Mexico a mere subsistence economy, each hacienda producing only enough — or nearly enough — for its own needs. Additional corn and beans, basic foods of the people since long before the Conquest, had to be imported.

Díaz was 80 years old as the end of his regime approached. Because of his lifetime habit of eliminating possible political opponents by playing them off against each other, he had no likely political heir. Ambitious intellectuals of the younger generation were becoming restless. Seven times the old dictator had gone through the motions of having himself re-elected to the presidency, and it seemed that he had every intention of repeating the farce in the election year of 1910.

Mexico's outward appearance of calm stability was compounded of wishful thinking on the part of foreign nations with heavy investments in the country, and the dictator's relentless suppression of those occasional brave spirits who dared to raise their voices in protest on behalf of the great majority of Mexicans whose wretched existence was driving them rapidly to the breaking point. Landless, yet chained to the land by debt and ignorance, millions of Mexicans were ripe for revolt. All they needed was a leader, a spark.

Francisco I. Madero, apostle of the Revolution of 1910, depicted by muralist Juan O'Gorman in Chapultepec Castle. He is escorted by cadets of the Military Academy.
Photo Joe Nash

The spark was provided by Don Porfirio himself when, in a mellow, expansive mood, he told a U. S. journalist that he was ready to step down and would, in fact, retire in 1910. This statement, of course, was intended only to impress U. S. readers with the genuine democracy of his government. But no sooner had the article appeared in print than it was translated into Spanish and given wide circulation in Mexico, amid general exultation.

Francisco I. Madero, a mild-mannered idealist and son of one of the largest landholding families in the state of Coahuila, became the original leader of the voiceless millions when he accepted Díaz' statement at its face value and announced himself to be a candidate for the presidency. Fittingly enough, he adopted the campaign slogan "Effective Suffrage and No Reelection," invented by the aging dictator 35 years before and then promptly abandoned.

Madero was no revolutionary, and this fact, combined with his slight stature — he was only 5 feet 2 inches in height — led Díaz to look upon him with tolerance. The enthusiastic reception given Madero during his campaign, however, moved Don Porfirio to have him jailed in San Luis Potosí until the elections were over.

On September 16, the lavish centennial celebration of Mexico's independence served to show the world that all was well and that Don Porfirio would live forever. It also acted like gasoline thrown on a smouldering brush fire.

Once Díaz' re-election had been proclaimed, Madero was released and, in October, made his way to San Antonio, Texas, where he declared the election null and void, assumed the provisional presidency, and called for a general insurrection to take place on November 20, the date since then observed as the Day of the Revolution.

Pro-Madero demonstrations in various parts of the country were quickly squelched and, at first, there seemed to be no real response to his call to arms. Disillusioned, Madero was preparing to sail for Europe when news reached him of an uprising in southern Chihuahua, where a storekeeper named Pascual Orozco and a fugitive peon, cattle thief, and bandit named Doroteo Arango, better known as Pancho Villa, on November 27 had successfully challenged federal troops.

Madero joined the rebels, and the Revolution of 1910 was on.

Perhaps in no epic struggle in any age have women played the heroic role they enacted in the Mexican Revolution of 1910. On foot, in freight cars, the *soldaderas* accompanied their men, foraging for food, preparing meals, loading rifles, nursing the wounded, bolstering morale, dying like the soldiers they were. *Photo Casasola*

THE REVOLUTION OF 1910

Probably a more confused struggle never took place. There was no one leader, but many factions all over the country, each with its own strong man. Sometimes they fought together, often they warred against each other.

On May 10, 1911, Villa and Orozco captured Ciudad Juárez, on the Texas border. In the southern state of Morelos, the dedicated agrarian leader, Emiliano Zapata, had recruited an army of villagers to resist the constant encroachment by the owners of large sugar-cane plantations seeking to expand their holdings. Díaz was persuaded by his advisers to resign, which he did on May 24. Two days later he slipped quietly away to exile in Paris.

In October, Madero called for national elections and assumed the presidency almost without opposition. Shortly thereafter, however, both revolutionaries and supporters of the Díaz regime, including Félix Díaz, a nephew of the deposed dictator, declared against him. General Victoriano Huerta put down several uprisings, then was named by Madero to command the Palace guard.

On February 18, 1913, Madero and his cabinet were arrested by order of Huerta. On that same date the Compact of the Citadel was drawn up, in the United States Embassy, by Félix Díaz, Huerta, and Henry Lane Wilson, the U. S. Ambassador. Under its terms Huerta replaced Madero as president and "peace" was restored.

At midnight on February 22, Madero and his vice president, Pino Suárez, were murdered "while attempting to escape."

The 17 months of Huerta's rule were a reign of terror. In the north, Villa commanded a strong force, and in Sonora, Alvaro Obregón, an intelligent, hardheaded farmer who was to become the real leader

A small *ranchero* in the state of Morelos, where he had watched the huge sugar cane haciendas swallow the lands of his neighbors, Emiliano Zapata was the natural leader of the dispossessed when the Revolution erupted.
Photo Casasola

of the Revolution, led another, composed largely of fierce Yaqui Indians. Venustiano Carranza, conservative governor of Coahuila, declared against Huerta, and joined Obregón. As these armies pushed southward, burning and looting, Zapata and his supporters in Morelos and Guerrero advanced northward.

Huerta was doomed, not only by the determined forces closing in on him, but also by the election of Woodrow Wilson as president of the United States. Wilson immediately recalled Ambassador Henry Lane Wilson, thereby closing one of the most shameful chapters in the history of U. S. diplomacy, and opened the border to the shipment of arms and ammunition for Villa and Obregón — their cost being borne by the Terrazas hacienda, from which Villa and his men rustled enough cattle to pay for them.

Obregón entered Mexico City on August 15, 1914. Huerta escaped to the United States, and Villa, enraged at having lost the race with Obregón, began a private war. Eventually, for a brief period, he joined forces with Zapata. They marched into the capital, compelling Obregón to withdraw.

At an opportune moment, Obregón struck back. Villa retreated to Celaya. Obregón followed and there, in April 1915, occurred the bloodiest 3-day battle in Mexico's history. Loading the remnants of his army into freight cars, Villa fled northward, tearing

Alvaro Obregón, Pancho Villa, Gen. John J. Pershing and Lt. George B. Patton, Jr., posed amicably after the U.S. sanctioned arms shipments to the rebels. *Photo Casasola*

up the railroad tracks behind him. Obregón's pursuit was relentless, but slow, for he repaired the tracks as he went. In Sonora, Villa's men were slaughtered by those under command of a grim-faced mestizo, Plutarco Elías Calles.

Down but not out, Villa returned to the border area. When the United States cut off his arms supply and recognized Carranza as president of Mexico, he gathered a small band of intimates and engaged in a series of raids and assaults. After stopping a train and murdering 16 American engineers, he raided the town of Columbus, New Mexico, in March 1916 — to force a local storekeeper to deliver arms for which he had already been paid. In retaliation, Wilson sent troops under General John J. Pershing across the border in pursuit of Villa, an ill-advised act that resulted only in making a legendary folk hero of Pancho Villa.

Carranza, meanwhile, was struggling to organize a workable government. The Constitutional Convention he called to meet at Querétaro in December 1916 was dominated by Obregón. Six weeks later, on February 5, 1917, the new Constitution was adopted. By and large, it was a confirmation of the one adopted on the same date in 1857, but with certain important changes.

Article 27 struck at the heart of the evils that plagued the country as a result of the Díaz regime. It declared an end to the hacienda system by proclaiming that the land belonged to the people and must be restored to them. It put foreign oil and mining companies on notice by stating, in unmistakable terms, that all subsoil minerals, including petroleum, belonged to the people and could be exploited only by Mexicans or by foreigners willing to recognize and abide by Mexican laws.

Article 123 was designed to protect workers. It safeguards the right to organize, to strike, and to bargain collectively, as well as to receive adequate pay, sick benefits, and other similar compensations.

In May 1918, Luis Morones organized, in Saltillo, the country's first national federation of labor unions. Known as the Mexican Regional Labor Confederation (CROM), it was patterned closely after the American Federation of Labor (AFL). The following year, CROM entered politics, nominating Obregón for the presidency.

But Carranza, despite campaign slogans, had no intention of stepping down. Adolfo de la Huerta declared against him in April 1920. Carranza fled to Veracruz, and was murdered in his sleep by his own men. De la Huerta served as provisional president until Obregón's inauguration in November.

Modern Mexico may be said to date from 1921, when Alvaro Obregón took the initial steps toward carrying out the social program of the Revolution, as set forth in the Constitution of 1917.

LOOKOUT POINT, MAZATLAN, SINALOA

Geographically, architecturally, culturally and socially Mexico is multifaceted, contradictory. Without altering its intrinsic character, it is also a land of progress, preserving the best of the old side by side with the new.

THE LOOK OF THE LAND

MAZATLAN, chief Pacific port on the coast of Sinaloa, has always been a paradise for sports fishermen, but now it is becoming increasingly important as a commercial fishing center as well, with plants for processing fish and shellfish for foreign and domestic consumption. Stepped-up activity is apparent in many ports on Mexico's 6,212-mile coastline, Pacific, Gulf, and Gulf of California. Thus a natural resource that remained relatively unexploited until 1970 is improving the nation's diet, providing employment and bringing foreign currency into the country.

In the Tarahumara Sierra, southern Chihuahua, is a series of six mammoth barrancas. Not the largest, but the best known and most spectacular, is COPPER CANYON, named by Jesuit missionaries who discovered a copper vein there in the 17th century. Its parallel cliffs appear to come together in places, as though to heal the 3,000 to 4,000 foot wound through which the Urique river runs westward, joining the Batopilas to form the Fuerte, key to the important agricultural area of northern Sinaloa and southern Sonora. "The Doves" is one of Copper Canyon's most impressive escarpments.

Said to be individually larger than the Grand Canyon of the Colorado, the barrancas unveil their grandeur to passengers on the Chihuahua-to-the-Pacific railway, which runs from Ojinaga, on the Texas border, to Los Mochis, Sinaloa. The railroad, an outstanding engineering feat, provides a view of part of the country that, despite its magnificence, illustrates why only 19 per

"THE DOVES" FORMATION, COPPER CANYON, CHIHUAHUA

LAGUNA VERDE CRATERS, SAN ANDRES, MICHOACAN

cent of Mexico's total area is even potentially arable.

Volcanic action is responsible for much of the country's theatrical scenery. In Michoacán, at the foot of the SAN ANDRES volcano, which last erupted in 1858, hot springs of sulfurous water bubble up to the

SANCHEZ MAGALLANES, TABASCO

surface. Medicinal waters at spas in many Mexican states invigorate the healthy and ease the pain of the ailing.

At a point where dense groves of palm trees came down to the shores of the Gulf along the Tabasco

LOPEZ MATEOS DAM, SINALOA

shore Hernán Cortés set foot on the Mexican mainland in the spring of 1519. Shortly before, during a brief stay on the island of Cozumel he had encountered Jerónimo de Aguilar, a Spaniard who, having been shipwrecked on the island 10 years earlier, spoke Maya fluently.

When they put in at a likely looking spot, now called SANCHEZ MAGALLANES, to take on water and foodstuffs, the Spaniards were unexpectedly attacked in force by Mayas. After several days of fighting, during which the invaders' horses and cannons were put to use, the Spaniards triumphed. As a gesture of good will, the defeated Indian leader presented Cortés with 20 slave girls, including an "Indian lady," Malin-tzin, later baptized Marina.

Less than a month later, when the Spaniards landed on the coast of Veracruz and were unable to communicate with the Aztec-speaking natives, Marina's inestimable worth was revealed. Aztec was her native tongue and in Tabasco she had learned Maya. She conversed with the Indians, then translated to Aguilar in Maya and he, in turn, translated her words into Spanish. Cortés' replies were transmitted in reverse. It was a time-consuming process but Marina's contribution was vital to the Spanish Conquest.

In the agriculturally rich state of Sinaloa, the LOPEZ MATEOS DAM has made it possible for an additional 315,000 acres to be placed under cultivation. All over Mexico dams are being constructed for irrigation purposes and to generate electricity.

Desolate beauty that exercises a special fascination is found in the northernmost reaches of the Mexican Republic. There lies the stony waste of the PEDREGAL DE LA RUMOROSA, so called because of the weird whispering, moaning and whistling of the wind blowing over and among the giant boulders that cover range after range of otherwise naked peaks stretching away to infinity. The only vegetation visible consists of scrub, maguey, and the ubiquitous cacti. Bizarre, and starkly dramatic . . .

PEDREGAL DE LA RUMOROSA, TECATE, BAJA CALIFORNIA

Its Indian Heritage

Nearly 4,000 years ago on the Gulf Coast, in the relatively small area of southern Veracruz-northern Tabasco, the OLMEC culture began to develop. From huge stone blocks the Olmecs carved colossal heads, stelae and monolithic altars. They devised hieroglyphic writing, a numbering system, a calendar, and made astronomical observations.

La Venta, at the mouth of the Tonalá river, was a principal Olmec site. When Petróleos Mexicanos (PEMEX) discovered oil deposits there, the enormous stone sculptures were rescued and transported to Villahermosa, for display at La Venta outdoor museum.

About 2,000 years ago, the Olmecs ceased to be an identifiable group, but their scientific knowledge and artistic achievements had been widely disseminated and exerted a notable influence on cultures evolving in Teotihuacan, Oaxaca, the Maya area, and elsewhere.

By 200 A.D. at TEOTIHUACAN, 30 miles northeast of Mexico City, the pyramids of the Sun and Moon

TEOTIHUACAN, STATE OF MEXICO

MAYA RUINS
IN LABNA,
YUCATAN

had been erected. During the century that followed, construction was accelerated and Teotihuacan became pre-Hispanic Mexico's largest urban center with a population estimated at 200,000. The metropolis reached the climax of its remarkable civilization about the middle of the 7th century but by that time Teotihuacan influence had spread over most of what is today the Republic of Mexico through a remarkable trading system.

On the northern plains of the Peninsula of Yucatán, the most brilliant phase of MAYA civilization developed after 500 A.D. Some sites, like those of Chichén Itzá and Uxmal, are partially restored, but one where little work has been done is Labná, on the western side of the peninsula. Named El Castillo, the structure on the left with its columned facade is largely in ruins, but the characteristic Maya arch that once connected two quadrangles is in an excellent state of preservation.

The intricate fretwork on the buildings at Mitla and the hilltop majesty of its even more famous neighbor, Monte Albán, are eloquent testimonies to the abilities of pre-Hispanic peoples in OAXACA. Recent archaeological work being carried on throughout the state of Oaxaca has produced new findings. The archaeological zone of Mitla, consisting of five separate groups of buildings superbly adorned, was once thought to have been Zapotec in its inception, Mixtec in its culmination.

MITLA,
OAXACA

However, it now appears to have been solely a Zapotec creation.

Above left is a corner of the Temple of the Columns Group. Right, the placement of the church typifies the early Spanish practice of raising churches on the site of Indian structures which they first destroyed. But in this case, possibly overcome by admiration, they refrained from demolition and built the church within one of the quadrangles that form the Church Group.

Its Religious Architecture

Probably the most notable feature of the Mexican landscape is the number and beauty of its churches. Those raised shortly after the Conquest often resembled fortresses with thick high walls. Their stark simplicity could almost be related in mood to that of the tireless missionary friars who labored long in the conversion of the natives. By the mid-17th century baroque was coming into vogue. Its century reign resulted in magnificent structures that were truly Mexican, no longer purely Spanish or Indian. Around 1740, an even more ornate style found favor, the ultrabaroque. Church facades were totally and intricately carved, and the interiors blazed with gold. The closing years of the 18th century brought a reaction embodied in neoclassic styles and the era of monumental ecclesiastical masterpieces came to an end.

Representative of the full flowering of the baroque, the ornate ZACATECAS CATHEDRAL was built in 1718, the third to stand on the site. Silver was discovered in 1546 and mines in the vicinity accounted for a large share of Mexico's total production of that coveted metal during the next 300 years. Wealthy miners were exceedingly generous in their donations to the Church. Earlier in the colonial period, Indian workmen built churches under the strict supervision of Spanish priests and friars, but by the 18th century, having become good Christians, they were given a free hand. This florid baroque, completely and unmistakably Mexican, was the result.

Also baroque, but in a different mood, is the exquisite facade of the CHURCH OF SAN FRANCISCO JAVIER in Tepotzotlan, state of Mexico, 28 miles north of the capital. The church dates from 1682 and stands at the southwest corner of the enormous monastery compound established by the Jesuits in 1606, primarily

SAN FRANCISCO JAVIER,
TEPOTZOTLAN, MEXICO
(left)

BELLTOWER OF
MEDALLA MILAGROSA,
MEXICO CITY (right)

to teach the various Indian languages to missionary priests. The deliberate asymmetry of the carved tower and facade, added in 1762, results in perfect symmetry. Restored inside and out by the government, the monastery now houses the Colonial Museum of Religious Art, and concerts and plays are presented in the church.

In the second half of the present century severity has returned to religious architecture with the construction of ultramodern places of worship of the concrete shell type, like the MEDALLA MILAGROSA (Miraculous Medal) in Mexico City. Its bell tower hints at the worshipful atmosphere that awaits parishioners, for the interior of the church is a gem of elegant simplicity, chaste, uncluttered. Springtime in the nation's capital means coral trees blooming in glorious profusion.

SAN JUAN CHAMULA, CHIAPAS

How Its People Live

The Mexican people and the places in which they live are as dissimilar as the country's geography and architecture. SAN JUAN CHAMULA, for example, is a Tzotzil village in the mountains of Chiapas. The primitive appearance of most of its dwellings is deceptive for its social structure is, in fact, complex.

San Juan Chamula was an important Indian bastion during the period (1867-70) when Chiapas was embroiled in the War of Castes that swept the Maya world; in that conflict the Indians vented their fury on whites throughout the Mexican southwest. As a corollary to the War of Castes, strange religious cults sprang up, curious mixtures of Catholicism and paganism. The church seen in the photo is the center of village life, but as the hub of a cult dedicated to the "Indian Christ."

CUETZALAN, a mestizo town, is located in the northernmost part of Puebla. Its climate at 3,200 feet is

CUETZALAN, PUEBI

semitropical, very humid, and it is the trading center
of an extremely fertile region where products include
coffee, sugar cane, barley, bananas, and precious
woods. Although it is economically important, because
it is off the beaten path Cuetzalan continues placidly
to observe traditional customs. The municipal clock
tower overlooks the palm shaded plaza with its lacy
bandstand on one side and, on the other, the sunken
area where the weekly market is held. Barefoot Indian

CITY OF
GUANAJUATO

women from villages back in the hills, wearing beauti-
fully embroidered blouses and with bright woolen
yarn worked into their high coiffures, gather there
on Sunday mornings to offer equally colorful merchandise for sale.

Off the beaten path, too—although in this case just
15 miles northeast of much traveled Hy. 45—is GUA-
NAJUATO, a colonial jewel of a city, and capital of the
state of the same name. The surrounding mountains

ACAPULCO,
GUERRERO

enriched the Spaniards with vast quantities of gold and
silver, and the city's steep, narrow, cobblestone streets
are lined with the luxurious mansions and magnificent
churches built or endowed by pious mine operators.
Today most of the state's wealth derives from live-
stock and agriculture

During its heyday, Guanajuato was as much of a
cultural center as Mexico City and the great European
operatic and theatrical companies of the 19th century
appeared there. In the 1950's students of the state

university began to present the works of Cervantes in some of the city's many small plazas. Today Guanajuato's Cervantes Festival, held annually, usually in early November, is internationally famous, and while the works of the great Spanish writer are still represented, the festival has been diversified with performances by symphony orchestras, opera, ballet and folklore dance companies from all over the world.

The glittering port of ACAPULCO — and this view shows only a portion of the western half of the splendid crescent shaped bay — ranks among the world's most popular fun spots, but nearly 350,000 residents, Mexican and foreign, actually live there the year round.

Acapulco provides a large share of Mexico's tourist income although other seacoast resorts have become equally important in the last few decades. Along the Pacific coast, Mazatlán, Puerto Vallarta, Manzanillo, and Ixtapa-Zihuatanejo have been developing rapidly. The newest Pacific resort, Huatulco, is farther south on the Oaxaca coast. The Yucatán peninsula has also been the scene of much tourism investment with new resorts on the Gulf near Mérida, and others on the Caribbean south from Cancún and Cozumel. Then there is Baja California which has long been a destination for dedicated fishermen; more facilities are in the making in the southern half of the peninsula.

One Mexican institution that stands firm in the daily life of the people, regardless of where they live, is the PUBLIC MARKET. The tianguis of Pre-Conquest times persists, with minimal changes, as the principal source of food supplies, household and agricultural implements. Even in Mexico City, with many millions of shoppers, it serenely holds its own in the modern world, despite supermarkets and discount houses.

All photographs in the foregoing section are the work of ENRIQUE FRANCO TORRIJOS, who dedicates himself to interpreting his native land in all her many moods and aspects. An aptitude for photography that dates from childhood has been refined and perfected through study and training in Munich, Paris, and Rochester, N. Y. As a student in the National School of Anthropology and History, he acquired a special interest in Maya archaeology that led inevitably to personal concern for the Mayas and Maya-related peoples, and his favorite sphere of action, sociologically and artistically, is the Lacandón area of Chiapas. His sensitivity and technical excellence make of his photographs true works of art.

Photo Anne V. Stenzel

PUBLIC MARKET, MEXICO CITY

MODERN MEXICO

Political Development

At the end of Obregon's 4-year term of office, violent uprisings greeted the election of Plutarco Elías Calles as his successor. The rebellion quelled, Calles took office in 1924 and established himself as a strong dictator. He furthered the aims of the Revolution, warred openly with the Church and, in general, ruled with an iron hand.

Calles had the Constitution amended so that, while a president could not hold office for successive terms, he might be re-elected later, and extended the presidential term from four to six years. Obregón, elected president for the second time in 1928, was assassinated three weeks later.

During the next six years three men held the office for brief periods. They were Emilio Portes Gil (1928-29); Pascual Ortiz Rubio (1929-32); and Abelardo L. Rodríguez (1932-34).

Through Portes Gil, Calles created, for the purpose of strengthening his dictatorship, the National Revolutionary Party (PNR). It included all groups of political importance and was supported, at first, by deductions from the salaries of government employees.

But Calles had misjudged the nature of his creation, for the PNR very shortly proved to be a significant step toward democracy; not democracy as the term is understood in the United States, but democracy of the type best suited, at least for the time being, to conditions in Mexico. All vocal segments of the population were represented in PNR councils. Political differences, therefore, could be resolved within the party, most often by compromise, and agreement reached on candidates and policies.

Until 1934, all presidents had been veterans of the Revolution, but products of the Díaz regime. The

Mexico City kindergarten pupils explore mysteries of educational toys. Strict birth control measures are now being promoted by the government; otherwise, by year 2000, children of primary school age will number 32 million. *Photo Yampolsky*

younger men, born of the Revolution itself, and with no adult recollections of the Porfirian Era, were impatient to assume leadership in putting into effect the reforms for which they had fought. To satisfy this growing discontent, Calles drew up and submitted to the PNR a Six-Year Plan calling for stepped-up action in the fields of education and land distribution, and the extension of government control over industry. He also suggested the name of General Lázaro Cárdenas, then 39 years of age, for the presidency. Both the Plan and the candidate were accepted, and in 1934 Cárdenas became president.

Calles was not long in discovering that he had again erred in judgment, and badly. For Cárdenas, the needs and problems of the people were of personal concern; the program of the Revolution, his creed. He took seriously the Plan that Calles had proposed with tongue in cheek, and wasted no time in carrying it out. In April 1936, when Calles' interference in government could no longer be tolerated, Cárdenas exiled him to the United States.

Without doubt, Cárdenas is best known abroad for his expropriation of the petroleum industry. On March 18, 1938, after the foreign oil companies that exercised exclusive dominion over Mexico's petroleum resources had refused to abide by the Supreme Court decision upholding a labor board's award of increased wages and fringe benefits to workers, Cárdenas announced to the nation, and to the world, that his government was expropriating the industry.

Equitable compensation being implicit in expropriation, long before agreement was reached with any oil company on the amount to be paid, Cárdenas was building a reserve fund for that purpose. Mexicans universally approved his courageous action to consolidate the country's economic independence, and responded wholeheartedly to his appeal for financial assistance.

No contribution was too small, no sacrifice too great. While women donated their jewels to the cause, school children all over Mexico were being issued formal receipts for as little as five centavos "toward payment of the petroleum debt."

By November 19, 1941, U. S. oil companies had settled for $32.5 million dollars, and in 1947 an agreement was reached with British interests. Their acceptance of $81 million raised Mexico's total oil debt to $113.5 million dollars. Every payment was met in full on the date specified, except that the final installment was paid 18 days in advance, on August 31, 1962.

In preparation for the 1940 elections, the PNR was completely reorganized and strengthened by the addition of new groups, and its name changed to the Party of the Mexican Revolution (PRM). It was decided that a more conservative man should follow Cárdenas, to give the country a breathing spell and allow time for the results of six years of reform to become apparent. The candidate chosen was General Manuel Ávila Camacho, who concentrated on industrial growth.

Since 1940 Mexico has been moving, slowly but surely, toward political maturity. There continues to be one dominant party (in 1946 it became the Institutional Revolutionary Party — PRI), but other parties put forth their own candidates and campaign for them. The ultraconservative National Action Party (PAN) is a perennial, sometimes sucessful contender, and a coalition of left of center groups is making a strong bid.

Like the old PNR, the PRI owes its strength to its constituents, who represent the gamut of national interests and their, at times, widely differing political viewpoints. Problems and programs affecting one state or section of the country are threshed out within the regional subdivision of the PRI, while decisions of a national character are reached by the National Executive Council.

Since 1946, following the completion of General Avila Camacho's term, all of Mexico's presidents have been civilians. They are: Miguel Alemán (1946-52); Adolfo Ruiz Cortines (1952-58); Adolfo López Mateos (1958-64); Gustavo Díaz Ordaz (1964-70); Luis Echeverría (1970-76); José López Portillo (1976-82); Miguel de la Madrid (1982-88); and Carlos Salinas, who took office on December 1, 1988.

In 1953, Mexican women were finally granted the right to vote; in 1970, the franchise was extended to 18 year olds.

Form of Government

The government of Mexico is very similar in structure to that of the United States. It consists of three branches — executive, legislative, and judicial — operating independently in the exercise of powers assigned to them by the Constitution.

At the head of the executive branch is the President of the Republic, elected for one 6-year term

Since the 1960's Mexico City has been refurbishing its historic monuments. In April, 1980 all such efforts were coordinated under the Historical Center Council, and work was accelerated. An important archaeological find was a section of the *Acequia Real* or Principal Waterway which, from Aztec times until the 17th century, served to supply Mexico City's downtown markets with products from southern lakeshore villages. Here, the restored canal is shown between the National Palace and the Supreme Court, a splendid sight illuminated at night. *Photo Anne V. Stenzel*

by popular and secret vote. His appointment of cabinet ministers is not subject to Senate approval, as is the case in the United States.

Mexico has no vice president. In the event a president should die in office during the first two years of his term or, for any other reason, be unable to serve, the Congress would name an interim president and call for national elections. If his incapacity should occur during the last four years, the Congress would choose his successor to complete the term without the holding of an election.

The legislative branch of the federal government consists of two houses, the Senate and the Chamber of Deputies, which together constitute the Congress of the Union. Two senators are elected for 6-year terms from each state and the Federal District. Members of the Chamber are elected for 3-year terms, each federal electoral district being entitled to one deputy for every 250,000 inhabitants. The minimum legal age for deputies is 21 years and for senators, 30 years. When Congress is in recess, a Permanent Commission composed of 15 deputies and 14 senators handles any urgent legislative matters that may arise.

As in the United States, the highest agency within the judicial branch is the Supreme Court. It is made up of judges appointed for life by the President of the Republic, who must submit their names to the Senate for approval.

Land Reform and Agricultural Growth

The most stirring battlecry of the Revolution was "Land for the Landless" but, when Calles took office in 1924, only 2.8 million acres had been redistributed among peasants in 624 villages. Some 320 million acres remained in private hands. Calles portioned out an additional 7.7 million acres.

Cárdenas made the first real attempt to break up large landholdings by distributing 45 million acres to three-quarters of a million families in 12,000 villages.

Nevertheless, at the end of his term in 1940, big hacendados and other individuals still held three times as much land as the *ejidatarios,* those peasants who work their small holdings communally.

Even before Cárdenas went into office, it had become evident that the mere possession of a few acres of land by the communal farmers did not provide a magical solution to the problems of the rural population. Land contributed to that solution only in terms of what it could be made to produce, and the average peon was totally unprepared to make the land produce. He had no seed, no tools, and no money with which to buy them. Furthermore, he was not a good credit risk.

It was to furnish the peasants with seed and equipment, to tide them over until their first harvest, that government agricultural banks were established. Once the crops were harvested, the banks acted as agents for their sale.

All subsequent presidents have continued to distribute land but, in addition, the government has placed increasing emphasis on teaching small farmers better agricultural techniques, the use of fertilizers, prevention of soil erosion, rotation, diversification and improvement of crops.

As we have noted, only about 19 per cent of the national territory is even potentially suitable for agriculture. Of that area, one-fifth is irrigated and the remainder depends upon rainfall. Thus, although "land for the landless" was the cornerstone of the Revolution of 1910 and one of the fundamental principles incorporated into the Constitution of 1917, an end to the land distribution program is inevitable within the near future, due to the fact that the amount of arable land is limited.

Agricultural workers, either possessors of small unproductive plots or those with no hope of ever owning land, poorly paid and then only seasonally, are flooding the larger centers of population, establishing semirural slums on the outskirts and creating urban problems of colossal dimensions. Many of them, too, flow across the northern border in an endless stream, generating serious problems for both the United States and Mexico.

It is estimated, for instance, that between 200,000 and 500,000 of these underemployed workers pour into Mexico City each year and the capital is faced with the hideous possibility of becoming a megalopolis with 40 million inhabitants by the end of the century. Many are the measures being taken to mitigate this prospect, among them, that new industries may not be established in the Federal District, and that some federal government agencies are being transferred from Mexico City to other areas of the country with a consequent resettlement of the work force.

The 1960 census divided Mexico's inhabitants (34.9 million) almost equally between urban (17.7 million) and rural (17.2 million), the latter figure including all those who lived in villages or settlements of 2,500 persons or less. In 1978, the government bureau of statistics estimated the division to be 64.9 per cent urban and 35.1 per cent rural, indicating clearly that the nation's demographic growth is coupled with an exodus from rural areas to already overcrowded population centers.

Land under cultivation in 1976 totaled 35.9 million acres, just about the same as in 1975 (35.4 million) but less than in 1965 (36.9 million). In that 11-year period (1965-1976) three of the 10 principal crops produced showed a steady increase: beans, coffee and wheat. Only in the case of rice and cotton did 1965 production exceed that of 1976.

Fishing, included together with agriculture, stock-raising and forestry as a primary industry, has made notable strides since 1965. In the coming years it should show steady expansion due to Mexico's imposition of a 200-mile limit along its 6,212 miles of coastline, thus protecting all its offshore waters from overfishing by Japanese, Russian, U.S., Cuban and

An Aztec pyramid found during excavations was preserved in the Pino Suárez station of the Mexico City subway.

other foreign fishing vessels, and also converting the vast fishing preserve of the Gulf of California into a private Mexican sea.

Education

Second only to his longing for a plot of land, once the Revolution of 1910 came to an end, the Mexican peasant wanted schools for his children.

It was in the field of education that Obregón made his most valuable contribution to Mexico's welfare, for he named José Vasconcelos as his Minister of Education. Vasconcelos devised and put into operation a unique formula for rural education which continues to be the basis of Mexico's educational system.

The task that faced him would have discouraged a lesser man. Education of the Indians and peasants had been almost totally ignored since the missionary friars worked among them in the 16th and 17th centuries. Not only had the opportunity of learning to read and write been denied them for more than 300 years, but they had also been deprived of the chance to acquire the most elementary knowledge of health and hygiene, sanitation, nutrition, civic responsibility, efficient work habits, modern farming methods — even a sense of human dignity and national pride.

Taking the activities of the friars as his guide, Vasconcelos organized a group of missioner-teachers who visited rural areas — by rail, car, horseback, canoe, on foot — surveying educational and health needs, enlisting rural teachers, studying local industries, and cooperating with the Ministry of Agriculture in the analysis of soils and the selection of crops best adapted to each area.

These pioneers, and the rural teachers they recruited, were missionaries in the truest sense of the word. The obstacles that confronted them were enormous. The Church bitterly opposed the establishment of federal schools, and many peasants were reluctant to disobey the priests. Large landowners preferred to hold their workers in ignorance, and their threats were often effective. There were no funds for buildings or materials — or for teachers' salaries — and, since normal activities of the nation had been suspended for 10 years, the teachers were untrained and inexperienced.

Only devotion to the cause, and a willingness to work long hours under the most primitive, sometimes dangerous, conditions, enabled them to carry out the program. By the end of Obregón's term in 1924, more than 1,000 federal rural schools were operating with 65,000 pupils in attendance.

These schools bore little resemblance to primary schools in other parts of the world. In addition to teaching children the basic principles of reading and writing, of personal cleanliness, of the regional arts and crafts, the teacher also instructed them in sports and dances, supervised the planting of gardens, formed orchestras, bands and choral groups, with the schoolhouse as the center of activity.

As though this were not enough, in the afternoon the teachers advised mothers on the preparation of food for undernourished babies, the use of mosquito netting, the need to boil drinking water. In the evenings, the adults of the community gathered at the school for instruction in agricultural techniques and animal husbandry, and for aid in filing applications to the government for the return of land.

Calles vigorously pushed the program set in motion by Vasconcelos, and by the early 1930's there were 6,500 federal rural schools and an equal number operated by the states or by private individuals. Education had been made available to 30 per cent of school-age children in rural areas. Illiteracy among persons over six years of age had dropped from 71 to 65 per cent.

Mexico's race against time in education has been sorely complicated by the mushrooming population, due partly to the success of health campaigns and the sharp drop in mortality rates. From 1930 to 1976 the birth rate remained stable at 3.5 per cent, or an average of 42.5 children born every year for each 1,000 inhabitants. By the end of 1982, it had dropped to 2.5 per cent.

Birth control or family planning programs were introduced, almost clandestinely, in the 1950's by private groups and international organizations and some positive results were gradually achieved. Now, however, faced with the need to import basic foodstuffs to feed the present population, in addition to providing housing, education, health services and employment for a steadily increasing population, the government has taken a firm stand.

On November 2, 1977, President López Portillo approved the plan submitted by the National Family Planning Commission to go into effect immediately.

The government provides basic structure and equipment for today's rural schools; local citizens furnish material for roof and side walls, as well as labor. *Photo SEP*

It calls for the reduction of the per annum birth rate to one per cent by the year 2000. Realization of this goal will depend upon adult education among both men and women in rural and urban areas, sex education for children and young people, as well as educational and health personnel trained to impart the required information.

In 1930 Mexico had 16.6 million inhabitants. Their number increased to 19.7 million in 1940; to 25.8 million in 1950; to 34.9 million in 1960, to 48.3 million in 1970, and in 1980 the population was estimated at about 70 million. A breakdown of the 1970 census figure by age groups is eloquent: children under nine years of age accounted for 31.7 per cent, those from 10 to 19 years of age, 22.6 per cent. In other words, more than half the total, 54.3 per cent, were under 20 years of age.

The problem of providing education for this ever-swelling flood of school-age children has been a staggering one; but the accomplishments of the various administrations since 1934 have been little short of miraculous. By 1950 illiteracy had dropped to 44 per cent among persons over six years of age.

Shortly after López Mateos assumed the presidency in 1958, an 11-year educational program was announced that contained some radically new features. Equally important, the funds with which to pay for it were provided. In 1930 only 33.2 million pesos were earmarked for educational purposes. The amount of 1.9 *billion* set aside for education in 1960 increased to 14.5 billion in the 1973 budget, and since then education has continued to consume a large share of the annual budget.

Under the 11-year program, a group of technical experts began to work on a blueprint for a rural school building that would be adaptable to all climates and all regions of the country, durable but attractive, incorporating the most modern materials and facilities. During the 1958-64 period, a total of 21,815 primary schoolrooms were built, every state benefiting on the basis of need.

Mass-produced in Mexico City of the finest and most resistant materials available, each unit consists of the metal framework, partitions, plastic window material, and desks, benches, and coat racks for 50 children, plus a blackboard with projection screen; projector with 50 reels of film; radio-phonograph with records; reference books for the teacher; work materials for the children; two sanitary units; septic tank or cesspool system; electrical installation and generator; and all basic furnishings for the teacher's home which occupies a portion of the building.

After its transportation to the locality where it is to be assembled, each unit becomes a community project. Local people furnish the best materials obtainable locally for flooring, walls, and roofing. Under the direction of government technicians, the townspeople perform the labor of erecting the building. Thus it becomes *their* school, a source of pride, and the way is prepared for the teacher to secure their interest and active cooperation in other community improvement projects.

The Anti-Illiteracy Campaign, begun in 1944 and designed for illiterate adults and monolingual Indians, has made it possible for millions of persons to learn to read and write. Instruction is offered in thousands of teaching centers, with the aid and cooperation of cultural missions, motorized missions and public reading rooms. By 1980 only 20 per cent of Mexico's citizens more than six years of age were unable to read or write, compared with 74 per cent in 1910.

Needless to say, the training of teachers to staff the ever-increasing number of primary schools with their burgeoning population of pupils is a matter of constant concern. Another aspect of the teacher-training problem is the preparation of technical personnel to staff the expanding number of vocational high schools and technological institutes. On the upper levels, the scarcity of qualified teachers is relieved to a degree by practicing professionals —lawyers, doctors, engineers, etc.— who devote their leisure hours, on a regular basis, to teaching their own subjects.

Indians persist in every state and, according to the 1970 census, numbered 3,156,616, of whom some 874,000 spoke no Spanish. But these figures do not tell the whole story, for the Indian census is taken on the basis of language spoken; hence children under the age of six are not counted. Also excluded are Indians living in regions too remote for census-takers to reach in the time allotted them. Therefore the real Indian population may be estimated at about six million, and it can be assumed that the bulk of children under six and many Indians of all ages, particularly the women, in remote areas speak only their native tongue, more than 50 of which continue in use.

The urgency of integrating that large sector of Mexico's population into the economic and social life of the nation is obvious. To that end, on February 24, 1977, less than three months after his inauguration, President López Portillo announced creation of the National Plan for Depressed Zones and Marginated Groups, to include all agencies previously working in the field.

By 1977 some 300,000 Indian children in 19 regions, or "areas of refuge," were enrolled in primary school under the supervision of "bilingual cultural promoters," of whom more than one-third held teachers' certificates. All these instructors are Indians, working with their own cultural groups: only Huicholes who have learned to speak Spanish work among Huicholes, only Zapotecs work among Zapotecs, etc.

The basic philosophy of the program is that, in order to become a good Mexican, the Indian must first learn to read and write his native tongue, and must acquire an intelligent understanding of, and pride in, the history and culture of his own group. Once that firm basis is established, he can then be introduced into the broader national culture without loss of his own cultural heritage and —equally important— without loss of identity and confidence in himself as a representative of that culture.

The primers consist of three volumes, all profusely illustrated in color. If the first is in the Otomí language, the second presents Otomí words and phrases together with their Spanish equivalents, and the third is in Spanish.

As in the days of José Vasconcelos, the promoters spend their hours outside the classroom working with children and adults in resolving community problems, encouraging local handicrafts, overseeing school garden projects —in short, doing anything that needs to be done to improve the living conditions of the people.

Public Health

Peaceful as Mexico appeared to be during the reign of Porfirio Díaz, the life expectancy of its people was only 27.4 years. Of every three children born, one died before reaching the age of one year. Sanitation and preventive medicine were almost unknown. Large segments of the population suffered chronically from malaria, intermittent fever, tuberculosis, scarlet fever and typhus. The country was ravaged by one epidemic

At a National Indian Institute boarding school students learn the ways of progress. *Photo SEP*

after another: influenza, diphtheria, bubonic plague, smallpox, cholera and yellow fever.

The normal toll taken by these and other diseases, added to the loss of life during the Revolution, reduced Mexico's population from 15.1 million in 1910 to 14.3 million in 1921.

The early Revolutionary governments were handicapped in their efforts to improve the nation's health by lack of funds, scarcity of roads and other means of communication, and the ignorance and superstition of the people. Rural schoolteachers were called into action, as we have seen, and medical students were —and still are— required to serve one year's apprenticeship in rural areas before being licensed as doctors.

Various governmental agencies were established and charged with specific duties in the fields of public health and welfare. In 1943, during the presidency of Avila Camacho, they were all united within the newly created Ministry of Health and Welfare.

Mexico's battle against disease and lack of sanitation, like the fight against ignorance, has been waged with missionary zeal. To what extent the battle has been won is evident in the tremendous increase in population since 1921, and the fact that, by 1982, life expectancy had increased to 68 years, compared to 27.4 years in 1910.

Smallpox has disappeared entirely, the last case having been reported in 1951. Deaths from malaria have dropped to the vanishing point, for the disease now occurs only in the most isolated areas; and satisfactory progress has been made in the eradication of other prime causes of death: gastroenteritis, influenza and pneumonia, tuberculosis, whooping cough and dysentery.

Hand in hand with the control of disease goes the improvement in sanitary conditions: safe drinking water, adequate sewers, government-supervised slaughterhouses and public markets, low-cost housing in both urban and rural areas.

Corn and beans continue to be the chief items of diet for the great majority of Mexicans, as they have been since pre-Conquest times. According to one prominent nutritionist, 75 per cent of Mexico's children suffer from malnutrition —not necessarily that they don't have enough to eat but that, for many reasons, the foods of highest nutritive value are absent from their diet.

This situation is undoubtedly due, in part, to the high rate of inflation that wracked the country even prior to the drastic devaluation of the peso on August 31, 1976. Food prices that were already beyond the reach of many people skyrocketed, making luxury items out of such important foods as meat, vegetables, eggs and milk.

Another contributing factor is the absence of medical doctors and health facilities in the more than 83,000 villages of less than 500 inhabitants that exist throughout Mexico.

To combat these and other problems the Ministry of Health has devised a program that, in addition to promoting the concept of family planning, will extend health services to this country's large non-urban population, encourage young doctors to establish their practice elsewhere than in the cities —where 65 per cent of all the nation's doctors now practice— and provide general health education with emphasis on proper diet for children and adults.

One of the most noteworthy achievements of the Revolutionary governments since 1943 has been the erection of hospitals and clinics, in rural as well as urban areas. During the 6-year period 1958-64 alone, 6,090 health units of all types and sizes were built, 80 per cent of them in rural areas. Since then construction has continued at a comparable rate.

The Centro Médico complex in Mexico City, with a separate hospital for each specialty, is operated by the Mexican Social Security Institute. Constructed 1955-61, largely with funds from the National Lottery, it was heavily damaged in the September, 1985 earthquake. Reconstruction has been completed and the restored complex remains Mexico's most important even though the decentralization of services and equipment that followed the earthquake will be maintained.

There are two forms of social security in Mexico: workers in general, and their dependents, are enrolled in the Mexican Social Security Institute (IMSS), while government employees enjoy the same benefits under the Social Security Institute for State Employees (ISSSTE). Together the two Institutes operate several thousand clinics and hospitals in every state and the Federal District, providing health care for millions of workers and their families. In addition, there are the many medical facilities of all kinds operated by the Ministry of Public Health.

An innovation on the Mexican scene is a limited form of individual health insurance available through the IMSS.

Economy

By 1940 the political state of the nation was sufficiently stable that goverment planners could turn their attention to industrial development. And the time was propitious.

Textile mills had been established in the 19th century. As mentioned before, under Porfirio Díaz foreigners were invited to exploit oil- bearing lands, work the mines, open factories. But after 10 years of civil strife, little industry of any kind was left intact.

Obstacles were legion. Any industry, to prosper, must have a market for its goods. The purchasing power of nine out of 10 Mexicans was nil. No industry can function without adequate communications and transportation media. Railroads were chaotic, rolling stock antiquated, routes insufficient in extension. Highways were almost nonexistent, and telephone and telegraph service in its infancy.

Despite these handicaps, industrialization was initiated. Progress was slow until 1941 when the United States, even before it was forced into World War II, turned more and more to Mexico for raw materials and finished goods it had previously secured from other sources by then no longer accessible.

Mexico's gross national product for the year 1970 was $33.9 billion dollars, representing an annual growth rate of 6 per cent, at constant prices, since 1940, and better than 7 per cent in the immediately preceding years. For 1976 the GNP rose only 2 per cent, the lowest rate registered since 1953.

What happened in Mexico during that 6-year period?

According to the 1976 Annual Report of the Banco de México (similar to the Federal Reserve System in the U.S.), the year 1976 showed a notable increase in the rate of inflation and a marked reduction in the rhythm of economic activity.

This situation did not blossom full-fledged in a single year, however, but was due largely to factors that had originated during the previous five years and were aggravated in 1976 by the appearance of new and disturbing elements, both international and domestic.

The sequence of events was, briefly, as follows. In 1970 there was an insufficient offer of basic products in the farming, energy and steel sectors, a fact that did not become evident immediately due to the contraction of demand in 1971. But when internal demand recuperated in 1972 and international activity began to regain its momentum, bottlenecks appeared that were translated into increased imports and reduction of exportable surpluses.

In 1973 and 1974 the increasing deficit of the public sector had to be financed to a growing extent by inflationary means, world prices rose, and the basic imbalances between increased demand and the insufficiency of domestic production worsened. These maladjustments were manifested openly in price rises and in a growing deficit in Mexico's balance of payments. Higher prices resulted in the loss of acquisitive power for large segments of the population. To these internal pressures was added the necessity to increase imports of petroleum and grain at a moment when prices of those products reached unprecedented levels on the world market.

In 1975 public spending momentarily rose to offset the depressive effects on the Mexican economy deriving from the contraction of world economic activity and from the uncertain behavior of private investment. Early in that year rumors concerning impending financial disaster and the imminent devaluation of the peso began to circulate. Private investors and corporations, Mexican as well as foreign, began to liquidate their assets in pesos, depositing or investing the funds abroad.

The outlook for 1976 was not auspicious. World economic activity showed an improvement, but the Mexican productive apparatus, already in a disadvantageous cost position with competitive countries, and with idle capacity in some of the activities related to foreign trade, could not meet the challenge. Within the country, higher prices and decreased purchasing power caused consumption to remain practically stagnant.

During the year the public sector accumulated a deficit of 124 billion pesos, compared with 96 billion in 1975. Uncertainty prevailed among businessmen, and the flight of capital not only continued but increased substantially. In general, all productive activities, with the exception of electrical energy and mining, registered growth rates lower than those of 1975. Finally, during the last half of 1976, when the banks began to suffer massive withdrawals of funds, it became necessary for the monetary authorities to support the banking system in order that it might cover such withdrawals without endangering its liquidity.

On the night of August 31, 1976, the axe fell. Since Easter Sunday, 1954, when the peso was devaluated from 8.65 to 12.50 to the dollar, Mexican politicians had taken great pride in proclaiming that the peso would remain pegged to the dollar at the 12.50-to-1 rate, even after the value of the dollar itself began to fall in the world's money markets. This was said to prove Mexico's "economic stability." Devaluation was not the remedy chosen in 1976; instead, the peso was allowed to float from an initial level of 20.50 to the dollar. After some months of fluctuation the exchange rate finally settled in the neighborhood of 23-to-1, but continued to float.

Even before the new administration took over the reins of government on Dec. 1, 1976, three months after the peso was floated, work began with the banking system to design a program of short- and medium-term measures to strengthen the economic and financial position of the country. The first move was to seek the cooperation of the International Monetary Fund, and on Oct. 27 the IMF approved support agreements for the balance of payments in the amount of $837 million dollars in special draft rights. That amount was to be increased to $1,068 million if and when Mexico upped its contribution to the IMF from $228 to $315 million, a step that was taken a year later. In the meantime, the U. S. Treasury Department and Federal Reserve System had authorized a short-term bridge credit of $600 million dollars to offset chaotic conditions in the exchange market.

It must be borne in mind that Mexico and the United States are inextricably bound together, not only by their 1,600-mile common border but also by their mutual dependence upon each other in many ways. During World War II, in addition to supplying quantities of raw materials vital to the U. S. war effort, Mexico interned enemy aliens who sought to infiltrate its neighbor to the north. Numerous U. S. companies established subsidiaries in Mexico after the war, developing the nation's economy, training workers and technicians, to the point that Mexicans now hold the top management posts in most of those subsidiaries. Approximately 60 per cent of Mexico's exports are purchased by the U. S. and the same percentage of Mexican imports come from the U. S. Tourism is one of Mexico's leading industries, and 90 per cent of its tourists come from the United States.

It is only natural, therefore, that U. S. banking and financial institutions should come to Mexico's aid in time of crisis, and they did so, as did international institutions and those of other countries. Huge loans were forthcoming from all these sources because Mexico's credit standing throughout the world had always been impeccable, and also because of the rapid development of Mexico's vast oil reserves.

In October, 1977 PEMEX, the Mexican petroleum conglomerate, signed a 90 million dollar loan agreement with 12 of the largest insurance companies in the U.S., the funds to partially finance exploration, primary production, refining and processing of petroleum. In November a consortium of 113 banking institutions in 11 countries, including both U.S. and Mexican banks, granted this country one of the largest unsecured credits ever extended to any nation, a 1.2 billion dollar loan to bolster the booming petroleum industry.

Oil, like gold, has always created excitement in human beings. In Mexico oil is nothing new, for it has been produced and refined since the era of Porfirio Díaz, mostly in the state of Veracruz. But when immense deposits in the southeastern states of Tabasco and Chiapas began to be developed in 1975-76, excitement rose to fever pitch. Exploration located comparable deposits in other parts of the country, for future production, and output was increased to provide a surplus of oil for export.

Profits from oil and its derivatives, however, cannot be regarded as the answer to Mexico's economic prosperity. There are many considerations not the least of which must be a drastic reduction in the birthrate, a continuing fight against inflation, and the restoration of reasonable purchasing power to the majority of the population — in the past 15 years working class purchasing power has decreased by much more than half. Mexico, of course, is not alone. The economic situation of the entire world, including the developed countries, appears uncertain. Mexico's fortunes are inextricably bound up with those of the United States. There have been and will be the continuing problems of "developed" and "underdeveloped," of the economies of the border areas, of illegal immigrants, of just plain working together. The "border" is not only a geographic division. It represents a deep gulf between national histories and cultures that only understanding and good will can even partially bridge, and there must be constant effort on both sides.

INDEX

(*NOTE:* figures in italics indicate illustrations)

114

BIBLIOGRAPHY AND SUGGESTED READING LIST

Aguirre Beltrán, Gonzalo, *La Población Negra de México, 1519-1810*. Fuente Cultural, México, D. F., 1946.

Bazant, Jean, *A Concise History of Mexico*. Cambridge University Press, London, 1979.

Caso, Alfonso, *The Aztecs, People of the Sun*. University of Oklahoma Press, Norman, Oklahoma, 1958.

Coe, Michael D., *Mexico*. Frederick A. Praeger, New York, 1962.

Díaz del Castillo, Bernal, *The Discovery and Conquest of Mexico*. Grove Press, Inc., New York, 1958.

Historia General de México (Four vols.). El Colegio de México, México, D. F., 1980.

León-Portilla, Miguel, *The Broken Spears; the Aztec account of the conquest of Mexico*. Beacon Press, Boston, 1962.

Lieuwen, Edwin, *U.S. Policy in Latin America*. Frederick A. Praeger, New York, 1965.

López Rosado, Diego G., *Problemas Económicos de México*. UNAM, México, D. F., 1970.

México: 50 Años de Revolución, Vols. II and III. Fondo de Cultura Económica, México, D. F., 1961.

Morley, Sylvanus; Brainerd, George; Sharer, Robert, *The Ancient Maya*. Stanford Univ. Press, Stanford, 1983.

Nicholson, Irene, *The X in Mexico*. Faber and Faber, Ltd., London, 1965.

Padgett, L. Vincent, *The Mexican Political System*. Houghton Mifflin Company, Boston, 1966.

Parkes, Henry Bamford, *A History of Mexico*. Houghton Mifflin Company, Boston, 1972.

Powell, Philip W., *Soldiers, Indians and Silver; the northward advance of New Spain 1550-1600*. University of California Press, Berkeley, 1952.

Soustelle, Jacques, *Daily Life of the Aztecs*. Weidenfeld & Nicholson, London, 1961.

Whetten, Nathan L., *Rural Mexico*. University of Chicago Press, Chicago, 1948.

Various publications of the Inter-American Indian Institute. México, D. F.

Various publications of the Banco de México, México, D. F.

Esta dieciseisava edición de A GUIDE TO MEXICAN HISTORY por Pauline R. Kibbe, se terminó de imprimir el 7 de agosto de 1991 en los talleres de Laboratorio Lito Color, S. A., Av. Pacifico 312, 04330 México, D. F., constando de 3,000 ejemplares.